SUCCESS
in
SEMINARS
&
TUTORIALS

A Guide for Social Science Students

Sukhvinder S. Obhi

OXFORD
UNIVERSITY PRESS

OXFORD
UNIVERSITY PRESS

Oxford University Press is a department of the University of Oxford.
It furthers the University's objective of excellence in research, scholarship,
and education by publishing worldwide. Oxford is a registered trade mark of
Oxford University Press in the UK and in certain other countries.

Published in Canada by
Oxford University Press
8 Sampson Mews, Suite 204,
Don Mills, Ontario M3C 0H5 Canada

www.oupcanada.com

Library and Archives Canada Cataloguing in Publication
Obhi, Sukhvinder S., author
Success in seminars & tutorials : a guide for social
science students / Sukhvinder S. Obhi.

Includes bibliographical references and index.
ISBN 978-0-19-902090-4 (paperback)

1. Study skills. 2. Social sciences—Study and teaching.
I. Title. II. Title: Success in seminars and tutorials.

LB2395.O34 2016   378.1'70281   C2016-900740-5

Cover image: © iStock/amaking

Oxford University Press is committed to our environment.
This book is printed on Forest Stewardship Council® certified paper
and comes from responsible sources.

Printed and bound in Canada

2 3 4 — 19 18 17

Contents

disciplines who completed my informal poll about what professors look for in student presentations. The results from this poll are an important component of the chapters on preparing and delivering presentations. I'd particularly like to thank Dr. Paul Maxim for valuable input regarding some of the sociology examples used in this book and thought-provoking discussions about university teaching. I am also grateful to Professor Henry Plotkin who was responsible for overseeing seminars when I was lecturing in psychology at University College London. Professor Plotkin is responsible for sparking my interest and appreciation of the seminar format, and his insights regarding how to effectively lead undergraduate seminars in particular have stayed with me over the years. I am very grateful to the five anonymous reviewers who provided extremely useful feedback on earlier drafts of this guide. Their input and enthusiasm for the project kept my motivation high throughout the process, and the suggestions they provided have improved the book substantially. I am deeply grateful to all the amazing students I've had the good fortune to teach over the years, from my time at University College London and Wilfrid Laurier University to my present academic home at McMaster University. I often feel that I learn more from students in my classes than they do from me. I am thankful to current and past members of the Social Brain, Body and Action lab for being an awesome team and for exemplifying many of the positive characteristics of effective groups that I discuss in the group work chapter in this guide!

On a more personal level, I could not have written this book without the love and support of my wonderful family. To my parents, Kuldeep Kaur Obhi (1943–2010) and Pritam Singh Obhi (1936–2014); you lived exemplary lives and taught us the value of education and helping others. You both are an everlasting source of wisdom and inspiration. I miss you deeply and I know you would have been thrilled to see this book published! To J and H, you inspired me growing up, and you always encouraged me to pursue my goals. To the two munchkins, J and J; you are like two sparkling little gems, and although you often make it impossible for me to work at home, you light up my life in untold ways. Your antics make me laugh every single day! I hope this guide might be useful for you both one day. Finally, none of my projects would ever get anywhere without my wonderful wife Ravi. Ravi, not only are you my number one proof-reader, you are also the most supportive, encouraging, and enabling life partner I could ever wish for. I would be lost without you. This book is dedicated, to you, J, and J.

Sukhvinder S. Obhi

McMaster University, Hamilton, Ontario, 2015

1

Introduction to Success in Seminars and Tutorials

So you've bought a guide on how to succeed in seminars and tutorials. Congratulations on taking the first step to improving your skills and achieving success in these types of courses! Whether you've done tutorial or seminar courses before or are about to start your first one, my hope is that you will find this guide highly valuable. This book is the culmination of my decade or so of experience teaching seminar classes to diverse groups of students in universities in the United Kingdom and Canada. If you've never taken a seminar course before, you might wonder what it actually entails. That is, what exactly is a seminar? The Oxford dictionary defines seminar as "a class at a university in which a topic is discussed by a teacher and a small group of students." A tutorial is defined as "a period of tuition given by a university or college tutor to an individual or very small group." It is rare these days for tutorials to be one-on-one, but they do happen that way in a small number of elite British universities. More often, tutorials are small group sessions with a professor or a teaching assistant in which students discuss topics covered in other parts of a course. For most undergraduate students, seminars and tutorials represent a change from the normal large group lecture courses that dominate university programs. They are characterized by discussion, individual or group presentations, and writing assignments, all of which are scrutinized by the professor when assigning a grade. Conversely, there are very rarely exams, although some professors will employ quizzes and mini-tests on occasion to help students stay on top of the material.

Despite the fact that seminars and tutorials are typically much less common than large group lecture courses, thankfully they *are* a staple component of many undergraduate psychology programs in the United States, Canada, and the United Kingdom. I say thankfully because I truly believe that these types of courses are among the most useful you will take at university. They offer an unrivalled opportunity to interact closely with your professor or teaching assistant and to witness how they think about the subject matter. They also offer the chance to interact with your peers in a relatively unthreatening environment that is supposed to foster critical thinking, communication skills, and a deeper look at ideas than is usually possible in large group survey courses. Graduate programs, in contrast to undergraduate programs, are characterized by their almost exclusive use of seminars and tutorial-style courses. This guide will be useful for both undergraduate and graduate students in the social sciences.

This short book was born out of the realization that students usually turn up to seminars and tutorials totally unprepared and unaware of what is expected of them. Over the years that I have been teaching small group classes, I've created notes that I've shared with students and that students have told me they've found helpful. These notes contained pointers about the various skills required in tutorials and seminars such as preparing and delivering presentations, writing a paper, and taking part in group work and class discussions. This guide is an attempt to collate these notes into a concise resource for students who are in, or thinking about registering for, a seminar course, or who are involved in small group tutorials. The emphasis is on understanding the key skills necessary to do well in these types of courses, and I have tried to keep the book relatively short, informative, and practically, as opposed to theoretically, oriented. There are chapters on preparing presentations, delivering presentations, writing a paper, working in small groups, and planning and time management. The emphasis is on students in social science programs including but not limited to psychology, sociology, anthropology, political science, economics, gender studies, and geography, although students in other programs such as life sciences and physical sciences may also find the information I present useful. It is my hope that, using this guide, students will improve their abilities significantly, and professors will reward this with better grades! I also hope that much of the material presented in this guide will be helpful after graduation when you end up in graduate school or enter the workplace. Many careers demand the key skills outlined in this guide, so with any luck, this small book will not end up gathering dust when you're done university, but will continue to be an easy go-to resource that you'll find helpful.

As an undergraduate student, your first exposure to small group sessions will probably be through tutorial sessions. In many programs, large lecture-based courses are supported by smaller "break-out" tutorials in which groups of up to 20 students meet, usually once a week, with an instructor. For first- and second-year undergraduate classes, these instructors are often graduate students. The aim of these tutorial sessions is to support your understanding of what the professor has been teaching in the larger lecture classes. You may find yourself given topics to discuss or a presentation to prepare and deliver to the class using PowerPoint or some other software package. You will probably be required to write some kind of paper that may or may not contribute to your overall grade for the course. The learning activities you engage in in tutorial classes are great for supplementing and supporting your learning. In tutorials you may also be given small group projects to conduct, and doing well in these sessions will depend on your ability to collaborate and function well as part of a small team. All the skills covered in this guide are highly relevant to most types of tutorial set up.

In contrast to tutorials, seminars are not usually meant to support a large group lecture course, but are stand-alone courses in themselves. Seminars afford students the opportunity to delve into a topic in much more detail than is usually possible in larger group lecture courses. For example, whereas most large group lecture courses rely on a textbook or course pack, seminars are usually based on in-depth reading of research papers from the literature. These are the kinds of resources that practicing researchers in the field use in their work. Furthermore, in many cases, seminar courses are not available until the third or fourth year of an undergraduate degree program. Thus, for many undergraduate students, especially in North American universities, enrolling in a seminar course is a big change from the more typical large-scale lecture courses that characterize first- and second-year undergraduate studies. These large group classes—which can have anywhere from 100 to more than 1000 students in a single lecture theatre—are usually "taught from the front" and are typically assessed by mid-term exams and a final exam. Some courses also include other innovative types of coursework, but this varies by professor. Further, exams are more often than not made up entirely of multiple choice questions, with little or no writing requirement. They certainly don't usually involve students giving presentations, or any significant amount of detailed class discussion. Although some professors do make an effort to get students talking, and the use of technology such as clickers to foster participation is growing, it is still the case that these courses are mostly defined by a traditional lecturing mode of content delivery.

Seminar courses are different on pretty much all dimensions compared to larger lecture-based courses. First, seminars are usually capped at a relatively small number of students: 20 is a typical cap, but it may be even lower—8, 12, or 15, for example. This format immediately introduces a new challenge for students. Now, the professor or teaching assistant can see each and every student clearly and close up. You can't hide in the crowd, and you can't get away with surfing on the wireless network while the professor or another student is talking (okay, maybe you can, but the chances of being spotted are huge). Seminars and tutorials are much more active learning experiences than lectures. In seminars you have to be engaged from the get-go! Also important, what is required of you in seminars is totally different from what is required of you in a large lecture course. Large lecture courses involve turning up, getting comfy, taking notes, and listening, again, with the occasional brave student contributing in response to a question the professor might pose. Sometimes large lectures may involve some interactive elements or demos and multimedia. There is usually no opportunity to write, although a few professors do introduce medium- and long-answer questions in these larger lecture courses. In stark contrast, seminars and tutorials usually don't involve formal tests and exams, but rather are assessed via individual or group presentations, some kind of written assignment(s), such as a research proposal or a critique of a research paper, or an in-depth essay on a particular topic. Within each session, you will be expected to contribute to detailed discussions on a specific topic. Sometimes a professor or teaching assistant will incorporate small-scale quizzes at the beginning of each class to help ensure that everyone turns up having read the material. There is often also an attendance and participation mark. Thus, there is virtually no single component in a seminar, in either style or assessment method, that matches what you encounter in a large group lecture course.

For many students, tutorials and seminars are not only different from large group lectures, but also very different from anything they would have experienced at high school. As a general rule, the level of independence required in university is higher than in high school. Students have to be proactive and take responsibility for their own education. There is plenty of help available but you must seek it out and not expect assistance to materialize whenever you need it. Similarly, no one is going to chase you to hand in assignments and meet deadlines; you'll simply receive a failing grade if you don't hand things in on time. Therefore, it is imperative to develop good time management and organizational skills in university and to get rid of any notion of depending on someone else to look out for you. University courses are more in-depth, and university educators must spread their time across hundreds and sometimes thousands of students. In addition, professors have research and administrative duties and are actually not full-time teachers (many undergraduates are surprised to hear this!). For all these reasons, the general degree of unsolicited input and guidance from a professor at university is lower than what most students have experienced in high school.

Another difference relates to feedback. Whereas high school teachers are often fairly generous with praise and positive feedback, many university professors are not. In fact, entering university students are often shell-shocked when they start to receive feedback that is not consistent with the feedback they received in high school. To be blunt, university is a harder, more competitive environment, where positive feedback and praise are often reserved for only the very best students (and sometimes even they don't get it!). So a key requirement is to learn how to handle what at times can be fairly harsh feedback. Rest assured, this state of affairs simply reflects the culture of academia—a culture that is geared toward fostering excellence. I recommend that students see a tough professor not as a person on a power trip, but as an honest assessor of academic performance. Professors might criticize your performance in class, give you negative comments on a written assignment, and be fairly damning about your level of understanding of a given concept, but I truly believe that, most of the time, this comes from a good place. Granted, not all professors are well versed in how to pitch negative feedback delicately, but more often than not, this feedback is aimed at making you better—so you can be the "best you" possible. This cannot be achieved without accurate feedback! I raise this point right at the start of this guide because tutorials and seminars are perhaps the harshest university classes in terms of receiving feedback. You may be called out for a contribution you make to class discussion, or receive a very poor grade on a written assignment. Having a constructive attitude and engaging with your instructor with the aim of self-improvement is by far the best approach you can take in these situations. In general then, university necessitates a much higher level of self-direction (coupled with much less hands-on guidance from instructors) than high school and an ability to take responsibility for your own outcomes.

All too often, professors or teaching assistants have expectations of students about how they should perform in seminar and tutorial-style classes, but they forget that students have never really been taught how to give a research presentation, how to deal with the inevitable nerves of presenting, or how to go about putting together a decent written paper. It is no wonder that I have heard students complain about harsh marks and unfair expectations in small group classes. I have been especially struck by the perception of a lack of fairness in marking, especially when it comes to participation marks, from students who are at the shyer end of the scale. I make a habit of talking with all my seminar students individually, and I have heard time after time that seminars are set up to favour the talkers—students who don't hesitate in putting their hand up and saying what's on their mind. While it is a challenge for professors to cater to the shyer students in a seminar class, I can't help but agree that this is an issue that has to be addressed. However, the key lies in both the professor taking personalities into consideration and students trying to move out of their comfort zone. There are concrete ways to go about doing this, and I will talk about these in this book.

Over the last decade, I have formed the distinct impression that students would benefit from some clear guidance about what is expected from them in seminars and how they can go about delivering on these expectations. So, my goal with this book is to provide students, who may have never encountered the tutorial or seminar format before, with some assistance to help them make sense of what is asked of them. I will talk about how to improve your presentation skills, your writing skills, your small group communication skills, and your time management skills. I'll also consider how to deal with the inevitable nerves of presenting to your classmates. The aim is to help you get the most out of your tutorial or seminar experience, including but not limited to enhancing your chances of getting an excellent grade.

Another key aim of this guide is to give you some "inside knowledge"—to tell you clearly what professors and teaching assistants tend to look for from students in these classes. Throughout the guide, I share my own expectations and the expectations I've heard many other instructors articulate. In being open about what professors are looking for, I hope to be able to help students hit the right notes and maximize their chances of seminar success, in terms of both learning and marks. The notion that learning and grades are both crucial considerations is important, and I want to emphasize it. Grades are one type of measurable outcome from a course, or indeed an entire program at university, but they are not the sole outcome. The other, perhaps more important outcome is the learning of new skills and the honing and sharpening of existing skills. In my experience, many students get so fixated on the grade issue that they forget about skill development and learning. It is true that getting good grades will help open the next door for you; but having good skills will be invaluable to you when someone invites you through that door. It will not be enough for you to simply aim for the right grade without spending time and effort in understanding the subject under study, and devoting time and effort to developing transferable skills like critical thinking, planning, and communication.

Consider for a moment, what is the point of going to university? We have all heard of the knowledge economy, the emphasis on high technology skills and innovation. I have heard it said that the aim of a university education is arguably to move students from being passive consumers of knowledge when they enter to active producers of knowledge when they leave. In this way, university should be a transformative experience that fundamentally affects the way in which individuals define themselves in relation to the world. The journey from being a passive consumer of knowledge to being an active producer of knowledge is an empowering one. My sincere hope is that this book can contribute to this process of empowerment by helping with the development of skills that are pertinent to knowledge creation and therefore also pertinent to the kinds of jobs you will compete for after university. Key skills like finding information using databases, extracting and combining ideas from this information, critiquing existing ideas and theories, communicating thoughts to stakeholders through both speech and writing, working in small teams and groups, forming and working to plans, and implementing first-class time management are all highly relevant to the jobs of today *and* tomorrow. These skills are valued by employers, and by honing them you will give yourself the best chance of becoming the most effective and sought-after person you can be.

Finally, because I know students all too well, this guide will be short! I have no interest in writing a rambling book that ends up being a lot of work to read for limited benefit. On the contrary, with any luck I'll be able to keep the usefulness-to-time-investment ratio as high as possible. This is not to undermine the importance of time investment—indeed, many of you have probably heard about the 10,000 hours required to develop expertise. While this idea may be an oversimplification in some respects, one thing is true: there are no shortcuts to achieving your potential. You need to invest time, but you need to invest it wisely. On that note, perhaps a really long introduction isn't the wisest use of time, so let's crack on with it. Have fun reading this short and simple guide, good luck with your seminar and tutorial endeavours, and please, feel free to send in feedback about things you found useful in the guide and other useful things that I can consider adding in future editions!

2

Preparing Presentations

The Most Fear-Inducing Part of a University Course?

I was standing in line recently at a campus café and couldn't help hearing the rather loud conversation that was going on behind me. Two students were passionately airing their fears and, I quote, "hate" of class presentations. As anyone reading this book will know, these two students are not in the minority. In fact, it's no surprise that a commonly used experimental manipulation that psychologists use to stress people out is to ask them do a short speech in front of an evaluative audience! Whether you're in a tutorial or a seminar class, there will almost certainly be times when you are asked to present something to the class. For most students, the idea of being judged, of "looking unintelligent" or of having an anxiety attack in front of everyone can be literally paralyzing. Nevertheless, this aspect of university education is a staple part of most social science programs. Far from being a testament to the sadistic side of university professors, presentation components are included in small classes because the ability to speak to a group of people is critically important in numerous occupations. Whether you end up as a project manager, a marketing

2 · Preparing Presentations | 11

professional, a management consultant, or a teacher, you will have to speak to a group of people at some point. In this way, you can think of presentation competence as a very useful "transferrable skill." Of course, if you attend graduate school and later become a professor or a teacher, you'll be speaking to groups of people day in and day out. Regardless of whether the idea of a presentation fills you with fear or exhilarates you (yes, there is a small minority of people who relish the idea of being the centre of attention), my advice is to think of presentations first and foremost as a training exercise for your own self-development. I'll talk more about handling anxiety and shyness in the next chapter on delivering presentations, but for now, embrace this opportunity to improve your skill set!

Common Types of Presentations

There are generally four types of presentations that you might be asked to make in a seminar course or tutorial, although other possibilities exist. Specifically, you might be asked to present a research paper, a research proposal, an overview of a certain topic, or a critical analysis of some material covered in an earlier class or reading. Obviously, these various types of presentations may necessitate the inclusion of different types of material and specific emphases. In addition, there may also be differences in time allowed that fundamentally affect the scope and depth of what you present. Common time frames for student presentations range anywhere from five minutes to 60 minutes and there is often some time set aside for questions and discussion after the presentation. When you are first set with the task of presenting in a seminar course or tutorial, there are three critical bits of information to consider right away:

1. *What* have I been asked to present about?
2. How much *time* do I have?
3. *Who* is in my audience?

You should always begin your preparations by asking yourself questions 1, 2, and 3 above. You need to do all the thinking and planning for the presentation with these three boundary conditions foremost in your mind. I unpack these three aspects in more detail below, to give you an idea of what sorts of things to consider.

What Have I Been Asked to Present About?

Sometimes professors are very clear about what they want from students in a seminar or tutorial presentation. It is important for students to make sure they understand what they have been asked to present. People sometimes have a tendency to interpret things in a way that fits with what they expected they'd have to do. Psychologists call this the confirmation bias. Be sure to avoid this bias. Once you've figured out what *you* think you've been asked to do, it's a good idea to approach your professor and get their explicit feedback on whether you've got it straight. I've seen students give amazing presentations, but in a way that doesn't fit the instructions given. The cause? They began working on the presentation before they'd reflected on task instructions and this ended up hurting their grade.

In some cases, your professor may be quite vague and give you lots of flexibility with respect to topic, purpose, and content. Students often feel frustrated, overwhelmed, and lost at a perceived lack of instructions and constraints. In fact, in my experience, students actually hate it when professors don't provide detailed instructions and guidelines. However, many professors take this "vague" approach by design, to give students the opportunity to really "own" their work and avoid a simple "follow these instructions for an A+" recipe approach. One reason students often feel anxious when professors don't give explicit instructions on what to present is that it is not obvious what constitutes a good or a bad topic or presentation. If you find yourself in this situation, you should speak to your professor. A hypothetical exchange with your professor might go like this:

Student: "I know you haven't told us exactly what to do to give us latitude to do our own thing, but I'm feeling a bit lost as to what would constitute a good topic/presentation and a bad topic/presentation. So I was wondering whether, hypothetically, if a presentation was on the topic of social inequality, and had the following components: definition of social inequality, social stratification, ascribed versus achieved stratification, unequal access to social resources including power, prestige, and relationships, which were delivered in an engaging and clear way, would it be the kind of thing you're looking for?"

Professor: "I think you're thinking along exactly the right lines. If you consider those issues and execute well, your presentation could definitely be great."

How Much *Time* Do I Have?

Although presentations can be from five minutes to 60 minutes in length, anything longer than about 20 minutes is rare for an undergraduate presentation. Graduate students may be required to do more in-depth and longer presentations though, and the expectations for these students are higher as well. As a general rule, once you know how much time you have, you need to figure out how long you can actually talk for, and still leave enough time for discussion and questions at the end. If you're lucky, your professor will have been specific when they set the work and said something like, "Presentations should be 20 minutes long and each person will have an additional 10 minutes for questions and discussion." If you're unlucky they'll have said, "Presentations should be about 20 minutes," and then leave it up to you to figure out how you use the time. As was the case with the "what" question above, if in doubt, ask your professor whether you should leave a few minutes within the allotted time for questions, or whether questions and discussion will happen outside of the allotted time.

Top Tip

Showing your professor that you've anticipated the potential issues involved in any aspect of your assigned work is a good thing. Even asking your professor a question about whether time for questions should be included in your planning paints you in a positive light. Professors always like to see students who are thinking ahead and considering their assigned work carefully. The fact that you've anticipated this potential issue and raised it with your instructor will be a plus point for you.

In their highly entertaining public speaking guide, Feldman and Silvia (2012) suggest planning to talk for only 80 per cent of the allotted time in situations where no explicit extra discussion time is available. This leaves 20 per cent for discussion and questions. This is definitely good advice. Whatever you do though, avoid going overtime. It's almost guaranteed that professors are including marks for timing, so bear this in mind, with a slight bias to finishing a minute or so early.

Who Is in My Audience?

This may sound obvious: your audience is your class, of course! Having said this, I have often found it useful to ponder over who will be listening and figure out whether my approach is going to resonate or not. Some really keen students I've seen sometimes make the mistake of ignoring their classmates and addressing their whole presentation to the professor. For example, they may make eye contact almost exclusively with the professor in an effort to impress. This tends not to go over well. Professors usually like to see that you are engaging your *whole* audience. Worse still, treating your presentation as a conversation with the professor can come across as contrived and make you seem as if you're sucking up to the person who'll be grading you. Don't do this! While it may not be possible to engage with each and every member of the class, you should at least plan on making an effort to address each section of the room as you talk. Another aspect to consider when thinking about who is in your audience is the background knowledge that group members bring with them. This is crucial so that you can design a presentation that connects with information they already have stored in long-term memory. Of course, within any group, there is a distribution of background knowledge ranging from those individuals with less relevant knowledge to those with more relevant knowledge. As a general rule, I usually try to pitch my presentations in such a way that the individuals with the least background knowledge will understand what I'm talking about. However, it is always a good idea to try to put something in your presentation that will appeal to the low *and* the high background knowledge individuals. One way of doing this is to vary the types of examples you employ. You could use very simple

Bottom Line

No matter what kind of presentation you've been asked to give (research paper, research proposal, overview of a topic, critical analysis), pausing to consider the "what," "time," and "who" questions, and asking for clarification from your instructor before starting your preparation, will pay dividends.

analogies to aid people with the least background information and more complex examples and explanations to satisfy those with more background knowledge. This way, you give yourself the best chance of engaging everyone and making your presentation personally meaningful to as many audience members as possible.

The next section highlights the case of presenting a research paper from the literature. Many of the recommendations are common to other types of presentations, so feel free to deploy appropriately for different kinds of talks.

Presenting a Research Paper from the Literature

Once you're sure about what type of content you are being asked to present, how much time you have, and who you'll be talking to, you can start getting into the actual groundwork that will help you plan and design the presentation. The very first thing you need to do is find the paper you have been asked to present. This may have been given to you or you may have some choice in selecting a paper on a certain topic to present. Choice is nice as students are often more motivated to do well if they've been involved in selecting the material. However, choice may not be available because the professor might have decided, quite fairly, that specific research papers provide the fundamental content that students in the class need to know. In other words, the professor may have just assigned everyone a paper to present. In this case the first thing you need to do is access the paper and start to master the material in the paper. We will get into how you do this in a second, but first let's think about the situation where you might actually have some choice about what to present. In order to select a paper effectively, there are a few things you need to be aware of about what professors generally look for in student presentations. I recently set up an informal web-poll for a group of 40 professors from diverse disciplines (including but not limited to psychology, neuroscience, sociology, kinesiology, economics, and anthropology). The poll asked about the importance they place on various criteria for student seminar presentations. The professors I polled were from different countries including the United States, Canada, England, Italy, and Israel. The results were clear, and I present the list of criteria in order of importance below. You can think of this list as being what the average professor is looking for in a seminar presentation:

1. That you have *read and understood the main idea and content* in the paper
2. That you have spent some time thinking about the idea and content—i.e., that *you have done more than a shallow read* of the document
3. That you have effectively highlighted the *reason* for the research, the *approach* that was taken, the *results* that emerged, and the authors' *interpretation* of the results
4. That you have some *substantive critical thoughts* around what the authors did right and what they could have done better—specifically, was the research design effective at addressing the question? Was the data analyzed sensibly and in an unbiased way? Were the conclusions drawn appropriate given the actual data?
5. That you were able to separate the *necessary details* from the less important ones and *distill only the essentials* in your presentation
6. That you *presented clearly*, used figures and graphs when appropriate (rated equally high with number 5 above)
7. That you *summarized effectively* and ended the presentation well
8. That you addressed the *whole class* and not just the professor
9. That you used your *allocated time* very well (i.e., didn't go too much over or finish too early)
10. That you have spent some time *anticipating questions*

Interestingly, professors gave the least weight to being appropriately dressed and to the appropriate use of multimedia demonstrations. As well as being an excellent resource for planning your presentation, this non-exhaustive list also provides clues about *what kind of paper* you should select. Often students will just pick a paper that has a title that sounds interesting. However, you need to go beyond consideration of the basic topic when selecting a paper and think about how understandable the paper will be and whether you can fulfill the (again, non-exhaustive) 10 criteria that professors will appraise you on, for that specific paper.

Where to Get Research Papers and How to Select a Paper to Present

Before you can do anything, you need to know where to actually get a research paper from in the first place. This sounds obvious, but I have met many students who literally had never been told where to search for and download research papers. In reality, there are multiple places you can search for and download research papers, and since this guide is primarily aimed at social science students, I will focus on where you can download these types of papers. Back in the day, we had to take a trip to the library (remember that old building?) and photocopy a research paper from a physical journal volume (can you imagine?). Nowadays things are so much easier. Your university library website should have a link on it somewhere that takes you to a list of available databases. Some of the main databases that social science students should be interested in are

PsycINFO: a searchable database with an emphasis on psychology and behavioural science—a social or developmental psychologist may use PsycINFO as their "main" database.

MEDLINE & PubMed: more medically oriented databases but with lots of psychology and neuroscience and neuropsychology content. As a cognitive neuroscientist, this is my main "go-to" database.

Web of Science: a very broad scientific database that holds content from numerous scientific disciplines from physics to psychology and everything in between. This is a comprehensive database useful for searching for interdisciplinary subject matter, for example "ergonomics" or "applied psychology."

Social Sciences Citation Index: accessed through Web of Science and covering many subjects within social science including but not limited to business, anthropology, health studies, political science, geography, and sociology.

Communications Source: a comprehensive database on mass media and communications theory, including linguistics and phonetics.

EBSCOhost Databases: a collection of databases from multiple social science disciplines, ranging from business to kinesiology.

Google Scholar: you don't need to access this through your university library—just type "scholar" into Google search on any computer connected to the internet. Google Scholar provides access to a great deal of content and thousands upon thousands of PDF files that are on the web. It's a great resource that I find myself using more and more.

These databases are searchable by topic, author, year of publication, and a host of other parameters. It is fairly easy to combine parameters in the search fields provided in these databases, and each database has built-in help that tells you exactly how you can maximize the effectiveness of the searches that you run. Usually, after you've typed in a query, a list of papers will appear. By clicking on one of the papers on the list, you will be taken to a page where you can see the abstract of the paper. The abstract is a succinct summary of what the paper is about, what the approach was, and what the main findings were. You should always start your consideration of a research paper by reading the abstract carefully. Reading the abstract will tell you whether the topic of the paper interests you and whether it fits with what the theme of the class is (that is, whether it hits the "content" constraint that you've been given, among other things). However, to make an informed selection, you need to access the entire paper. Most university library database search results have a link you can click to access the whole paper. Once you've accessed the paper (usually as a PDF or

HTML), you can look over the paper and decide if it's a good one to pick for your presentation. Some important questions to consider when making this determination are:

1. Is the topic interesting and relevant to the course?
2. Do I understand why the research was done? Is there a clear research question and is it well motivated?
3. Do I understand what the authors did? How they conducted the experiment(s) or research process?
4. Do I understand why and how they measured what they measured?
5. Do I understand the data that they present? Do the graphs/ figures and tables make sense?
6. Will I be able to critique the paper effectively? Are there aspects of the paper that I think could have been done better?
7. Will I be able to summarize the paper effectively and clearly?

Many of these self-directed questions resemble the things that professors look for, as outlined in my poll results. What you are doing with these self-directed questions is figuring out if the paper is accessible to you (even with some effort!), and whether you feel capable of disseminating the research to your peers and providing critical analyses. If, for example, the paper has very complex statistical or methodological procedures that you are not familiar with and that you don't feel that you would be able to learn in time for the presentation, it may not be the ideal paper to select.

Bottom Line
Don't just consider the topic of the paper when selecting it—consider whether you will be able to do a good job of presenting and critiquing it clearly in the time allowed.

Reading the Paper: The Flexi Method
So, once you've identified a paper, you'll be faced with the task of actually reading it in preparation for your presentation (or assignment). Many students are quite overwhelmed when they're

first exposed to primary research sources like peer-reviewed papers. I have heard students saying that they had no idea where to begin when they were first confronted with reading a paper. So, where should you start? One approach could be to start at the beginning and read the paper start to finish. You could do this multiple times (as needed), but in my experience, this approach is inefficient and increases the chances that you'll get lost, impatient, and frustrated.

Over the years, I have developed what I think is a more efficient approach to reading papers. I call it the Flexi Method because it is a flexible way of reading efficiently in a task-dependent manner. What do I mean by "task-dependent manner"? Clearly, when you read a paper, you usually have some goal or task at hand that you are working on. Depending on the task, your approach might be different. Thus, you have to be *flexi*ble in how you go about things. For example, on one hand, as is the focus in the current chapter, you might be reading a paper so that you can put together an in-depth presentation about it. In such a case, you will need to study the paper and essentially know it inside out. On the other hand, you might be reading a paper to find out something specific about a method, or simply to provide an additional reference for something you have written, or in some cases just to double-check that what you remember about the paper is correct. In these cases, you need to understand the paper, but you may not need to know the paper in the same detail as you would need to know it for a presentation. This is where the Flexi Method comes in. The Flexi Method holds that your strategy can range from simply reading the abstract once to reading the whole paper multiple times, depending on the task at hand. In most circumstances, the minimum number of "looks" you need to give a paper, even just to get the gist, is two. Why? Because with only one look, you might misread something and consequently misinterpret information. A second look is *necessary* to make sure that what you thought you read during the first look is actually what is written in the paper! There is an exception though—this is the situation where you are simply refreshing your memory of a paper or doing a quick and cursory overview of many studies using a database. In such a case, reading just the abstract of the paper may be sufficient, at least until a later time.

Assuming you're doing more than a single read of the abstract, the *Flexi Method involves sequential surface reading followed by deeper reading of the paper.* I recommend two surface reads to start, followed by multiple deep reads depending on your task. For example you may need five (or more) reads if, for example, your goal is to completely understand the theoretical context, methods, data, and interpretation of results in the paper. Clearly, this can (and should) require considerable time investment. Don't be fooled into thinking that understanding social science papers is quick!

Below I break down the different levels of reading involved in the Flexi Method.

First Look: The Surface Read
1. Read the title and abstract.
2. Read the introduction—read the first couple of paragraphs carefully, then skim read the remaining paragraphs until you get to the hypothesis formation (usually one or two paragraphs right before the methods section). During skim reading you may have to stop and ponder important points that you come across.
3. Skim read the methods but focus on extracting the experimental design—what was manipulated and how? What was measured?
4. Look at the figures and graphs—what do they show? How do they relate to the hypotheses?
5. Read the first two paragraphs of the discussion and skim read the remaining paragraphs until the final two paragraphs, which again should be read carefully (the ending gives you an idea of the take-home message—usually!)

At the end of this first process you should have a pretty good feel for the following points:

1. What motivated the research: this is the "gap" in knowledge that the paper was trying to address.

2. The exact research question: how did the authors articulate the "gap" as a research question?
3. The experimental design: how did the authors turn the question into an empirical study?
4. The main result: were the hypotheses supported or rejected?
5. How the authors tied the results to the main question of the paper: where does the paper fit within the broader theoretical context?

Second Look: The Below-Surface Read

The second look involves a repeat of the first look process, but with a more thorough read. Pay particular attention to the methods and results section in this second read—you really need to be sure of what was *actually* done. Alternatively, if you only need to use the paper as a secondary reference for something you're working on, you can skim through again, with a focus on making sure your understanding from the first look is accurate (that is, make sure you didn't totally misinterpret or misunderstand the paper the first time round). At the end of the second look, you should have a pretty good feel for what the authors were trying to achieve and the theoretical context of the work, as well as how the data were collected and how they fit into the theoretical context to advance knowledge. For many tasks, such as finding a reference for a point you are making in a paper, or forming part of a broader literature review, this *two-look method* is adequate.

Deep Reading: Subsequent Looks Require Critical Analysis and Perspective Switching

For some tasks, like preparing for a presentation, or doing a comprehensive written critique of a paper, *two looks is not enough*. You will likely need at least another one to three reads of the paper during which you should focus on critical appraisal. You often hear this term, but *how do you* actually critically appraise something? One method I find useful while reading papers involves "flipping" between the experimenter's perspective and my own perspective on their work. For example, when doing this, you might ask yourself: "Why did the approach make sense to the experimenter, given the theoretical context they provided?" You might then ask:

"Does the approach make sense to me?" Put another way, you should be constantly asking yourself: "What was the experimenter thinking when they decided to take X approach?" Followed by: "Given the same context, would I have taken that approach or a different one, and why?" In my opinion, this process of estimating the experimenter's perspective and comparing this with your own perspective on the work is the foundation for critical appraisal. To underline this point: by putting yourself into the experimenter's shoes and then your own shoes as you study the paper for the third and fourth times (or more), you can determine whether there are any major areas of discordance. Is there something the

---

Surface Read (~5–20 minutes needed)

- Title and Abstract—What's the gist?
- Introduction—Motivation for study, question, hypotheses?
- Skim Methods—Understand study design; is it appropriate?
- Look over figures/graphs—Main result(s); do they make sense?
- Discussion—How did authors interpret the data; does it make sense?

Below-Surface Read (~20–60 minutes needed)

- Did I get it right?—repeat Surface Read to ensure accuracy OR
- Read through with greater care to more fully understand details

Deep Read (1+ hours needed)

- Read with care; focus on arguments and reasons. For each paragraph:
  - What was author thinking and would I think the same way given the same information?
  - Are ideas supported with solid evidence?
  - Consult other sources to understand and cross-check the details, assumptions, and premises
  - Consider differences between your opinion and authors' opinion, and any identified poor reasoning by author(s) to critically appraise their work

---

Figure 2.1 Flexi Approach to Reading Papers

experimenter did, or an assumption they made, or a set of reasons they used to justify their thinking that you just don't get or don't agree with? These discordances are the sorts of things you can then include in your own presentation or assignment.

What the perspective-switching approach helps you to do is to *deconstruct the arguments made by the researchers, and determine whether they make sense from your point of view.* Arguments are nothing more than ideas supported by reasons. Your task when critically appraising a research paper (or any other form of argument) is essentially to analyze the reasons supporting the ideas—that is, the reasons that supposedly justify the argument(s) being made.

To make this concrete, imagine an argument in a social psychology paper about how feeling powerful affects behaviour. The researchers suggest that power will increase the likelihood that people will cheat on an experimental test. The reasons they use to justify this idea are that power increases the tendency for people to underestimate risk and to engage in more risky behaviour. On the surface, these seem like plausible reasons to justify their prediction. However, there is other research showing that power actually accentuates peoples' more enduring tendencies. So if a person is very ethical under normal circumstances, power would amplify their good ethics, thus making them less likely to cheat. With this information in mind, what appeared to be a reasonable idea in the first instance now looks a little shaky. In this case, the authors provided a limited subset of reasons for their idea, while ignoring other reasons that might have led to the opposite prediction. This example highlights two important aspects of critical appraisal. First, your appraisal skills get better the more information you have at your disposal, which means you need to be as educated as you can be about a topic (no shortcuts here, you just need to spend time on the topic). Second, you should be on guard for biased presentation of reasons to support arguments. This second issue crops up all the time in social science. Sometimes, people launch their research from a biased perspective and seek confirmatory information. This so-called confirmation bias is often unconscious and is extremely dangerous as it undermines a basic tenet of the scientific method—that conclusions should be drawn from an unbiased examination of the evidence.

Consider another hypothetical example of a dubious argument for which the reason given doesn't justify the conclusion. Imagine a news story about a famous sports star who assaulted a fan. The story claims that stardom leads to feelings of power and that power causes people to act aggressively. While this sounds somewhat plausible, the whole argument falls down when you consider that there are thousands of other powerful individuals who do not assault people. Thus, there must be something else going on: other variables that perhaps interact with power to facilitate aggressive behaviour. In this way, you can quite easily conclude that the reasoning put forward in the news story is not adequate justification for the argument being made.

The bottom line, then, is that when reading papers, for every point or idea raised and for every conclusion drawn by the authors, you should identify the reasons they provide and analyze these reasons to determine whether they are sensible. Your ability to do this well will improve as you acquire more information about the topic under study. The more you know, the better you'll be at situating the presented ideas (and reasons) in the context of other information on that topic.

Bottom Line

If nothing else, when reading a paper keep an eye out for biases, and read skeptically; ask yourself at every juncture why you should "buy" what the authors are saying. Put another way, don't assume that anything being said is credible. Rather, look for solid evidence for credibility. Bringing a skeptical mindset and a willingness to think hard about what you are reading is the foundation of strong critical appraisal.

In addition to these general principles of critical appraisal, when applying the Flexi Method, you will also want to ask specific questions about the research as you read. Here's a 10-point checklist of things to think about specifically as you go through the paper after the surface read(s):

1. What was the *reason* the research was done?
2. What was the specific research *question*?

3. How exactly did the authors address this question; what was the *study design, including identification of independent variables*?
4. What *dependent variables* were measured?
5. How did the authors *analyze the data*?
6. Does the *presentation of data* clearly illustrate the effects of interest?
7. Do the *conclusions* in the paper make sense given what the data show?
8. Are there potentially *extraneous, confounding variables* in addition to the variables of interest, and have the authors done enough to rule out their effects?
9. Could the authors have addressed the question in *any other, better* ways?
10. What is *your* overall opinion about the *strengths and weaknesses* of the paper and the *contribution to knowledge* that it makes?

You can use points 1–10 above as headings and jot down your thoughts about each question. You can even use these 10 points in a mind map to organize your thoughts. Again, you will likely have to read the paper several times to get a thorough understanding of what it is about. Of course, if you have trouble understanding any aspect of the paper, go and see your professor. However, and this is important, *before* you do this, you have to be aware that, if you go to see your professor unprepared, having only half-heartedly tried to understand the issues, you run the risk of creating a negative bias in the mind of the professor.

Top Tip

When you approach your professor with questions, if they see that you have been tenacious in trying to understand the material and that you have specific, very focused questions, you end up creating a positive bias. Despite the fact that professors may not intentionally judge you on anything other than your presentation on the day, human beings have a tendency to form unconscious impressions.

A Quick Note on Research Proposal Presentations

One type of presentation that is quite common in seminars is the research proposal presentation. Many of the tips and guidelines provided above also apply to this type of presentation. However, there are some key differences and specific things to consider for this type of presentation. If tasked with putting together a research proposal presentation, try bearing the following 10 points in mind:

1. Introduce the topic and the area of study.
2. Identify the gap in knowledge—what's the best way to do this? Does it logically flow from 1 above?
3. Identify a question that would help to address the gap in knowledge.
4. Come up with an experiment that can effectively answer the question.
5. Provide a clear statement of your experimental hypothesis.
6. Outline the experimental design. What are you manipulating? What are the independent and dependent variables? What are you measuring?
7. Describe your method: outline the details, number of trials, counterbalancing, participant demographics, and other details of equipment and approach.
8. Outline the expected results and present "projected" graphs or tables.
9. Relate these results back to the hypothesis and interpret what these results mean and how they help fill the gap in knowledge.
10. Outline the limitations of your approach and suggest avenues and ideas for future research.

Considering these additional 10 points when putting together a research proposal presentation, in conjunction with the guidelines below, should be efficacious for helping you put together an amazing proposal presentation.

Planning Your Presentation

Whether you are tasked with doing a paper presentation, a proposal presentation, or any other kind of presentation, there are other important considerations that you might find useful. I highlight some of these below.

Consider the "Peak and End Rule" and the "Primacy and Recency" Effects

The peak and end rule is interesting to know about and relates to how people remember an episode or series of episodes. Before describing it, I warn against using it or any other "rule" as a magic bullet or as a guarantor of success. Essentially, the rule states that, when people think back about an experience, they tend to base their overall impression on two moments: the moment of peak affect and the affect at the end of the experience. In their landmark paper, Frederickson and Kahneman (1993) found that an average of affect experienced at these two moments accounted for 94 per cent of the variance in the overall evaluation of an affective experience. What does this mean? Certainly not that the beginning of your presentation doesn't matter. Rather, I would suggest that consideration of the peak and end rule emphasizes that you should think about the moments you are "creating" in your talk for your audience. A good talk, arguably, will be one in which as many people in the audience as possible experience a strong positive affective moment and a strong ending. Said another way, a good talk should create the greatest likelihood of having content that is personally meaningful to as many people in the audience as possible. Again, consideration of this rule is not given here as a prescription, but rather as food for thought. While the peak and end rule pertains to the affective aspects of experiences, in regards to memory performance, research shows that individuals remember the first and the most recent information presented to them better than the information in between. Given these so-called primacy and recency effects, it is useful to consider ways in which you can make your beginning and ending as strong, engaging, and inclusive of key information as possible. Indeed, in his excellent book on presentations, the Stanford cognitive psychologist Stephen Kosslyn recommends using sections and putting the most important information at the beginning or at the end of each section (Kosslyn, 2007).

A Strong Beginning

What is a strong beginning? For all practical purposes it is a beginning that grabs your audience members' attention and piques their interest. How can this be achieved? Well, think about it: what do you think the majority of your audience members will be captured by when it comes to your paper? In the social sciences, due to the relatable nature of much of the subject matter, it is often relatively easy to "hook" the audience early on with an opening statement, remark, or question. Indeed, compared to more abstract disciplines like certain topics in physics and mathematics, creating an appealing beginning is arguably a breeze for social science students.

One way to grab the audience's attention is to be slightly controversial or "edgy" at the start of your presentation. This can create intrigue and pull the audience's attention and motivate them to listen to what you're saying. For example, if your paper is about attitudes toward immigration as a function of socio-economic status, you could begin by saying something such as, "Have you ever wondered why some people are just so anti-immigration?" This kind of beginning could be good because it is slightly edgy and because everyone has probably met someone who is not a fan of immigration, so your remark is personally meaningful and creates anticipation of where you're going next. You could present a cartoon, in conjunction with a statement like this, to increase the impact of your opening remarks. This kind of opening could be followed by saying something along the lines of, "Well, Smith and Collins are two people who do wonder about this, in fact so much so, that they decided to do this study to tease apart how people from different socio-economic strata think about immigration...." If you don't want to be controversial or edgy, you might want to consider starting by changing the flow of what's been going on prior to your talk. People will pay attention to events that deviate from the norm.

1

(Bad opening, example slide)

Police Violence in NYC

- More than 1100 people in NYC had choke holds used on them between 2000 and 2014 by NYPD officers

- Eric Garner was choked to death in 2014 by an officer of the NYPD

- Garner had been in trouble for petty offences

- He was asthmatic and repeatedly said he couldn't breathe

- Officer responsible was not indicted

2

(Good opening, first slide)

The Issue

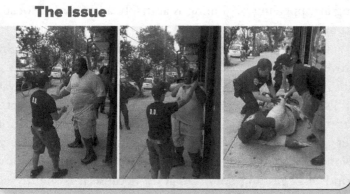

Figure 2.2 Bad and Good Opening Slides
(1) is an example of a bad opening slide. (2) is the first of two slides in an example of a good

A Compelling Middle

I believe that each slide should convey from one to three important ideas, so bear this in mind as you talk—highlight the point(s) for your audience and repeat key concepts and ideas. If you shoot for three ideas, you'll be within the capacity limits of working memory and will therefore give your audience a good chance to integrate the information with pre-existing knowledge in long-term memory,

Slide notes:

- Eric Garner—a man who had been in trouble for petty offences
- Died in July 2014
- NYPD officer choked him to death
- He was asthmatic and had a heart condition
- He repeatedly said he couldn't breathe
- Police officer was not indicted
- 2009–2014 more than 1100 reports of officers using chokeholds in NYC
- Why do we know?
- It was all caught on video

3

(Good example, second slide)

What if this was your father?

4

opening. (3) are the speaking notes that go with the first slide. (4) would follow the first slide after you reached the end of your notes.

which is exactly what you want. Plan on talking for one or two minutes per slide, possibly longer for slides presenting complex ideas. Consider summarizing at the end of every section (a section could be a few slides long) with a statement similar to, "So, just to summarize so far, the authors came into this study thinking *XYZ*, because of *ABC*." This is not always possible or appropriate, but it can help people separate the details you may have mentioned from the main take-home message of the section. Within sections of a presentation, ideas presented on one slide should build on what was presented on previous slides, until you start a new section, which can then focus on a different set of ideas. Plan on verbally *bridging* one slide to the next so that audience members are never left trying to connect the ideas of successive slides without some guidance from you! This last point refers to the efficacy of cues to help people attend to the right information. Imagine you've gone to meet a friend of a friend at a train station but you've never met this person. Your friend showed you a photo but it was old and probably isn't going to be much good. The train pulls in, people get off, and the crowd comes rushing toward you. You are scanning the scene trying to form some kind of match with the old photo you've seen, not really sure who you're looking for. What a nightmare! Now imagine your friend calls you just before the train pulls in and says, "Hey, I just talked to Judy and she said she's wearing a waist-length red jacket and is carrying a light blue bag." Now, your job is so much easier. In psychological terms, you've now been provided with a good *cue* to help you pay attention to the relevant parts of the scene. Likewise, in a presentation, even a brief word about what audience members need to be thinking about can help them attend to and organize the information you present in a much better way. I recently attended an excellent presentation in which the presenter excelled at this skill. At the start of each slide she'd make a comment along the lines of, "What I want you to pay attention to on this slide is the sharp increase in the number of items remembered in test X compared to test Y." This simple "heads up" or cueing allowed audience members to focus on exactly the most relevant aspect of the slide and not the less crucial information that was also present.

One common mistake students make in presentations is trying to say too much or use language that is not conversational in style. This often happens when students have written themselves a script and are simply reading from it. It is easier for people to digest small chunks of information presented using simple language, so make sure your manner of speaking is to the point and not too long-winded. For example, if you are a psychology or neuroscience student and are explaining what the motor cortex is, you wouldn't want to say:

The motor cortex is a region of the cerebral cortex that lies anterior to the central sulcus, which itself is just anterior of the somatosensory cortex. Lesions to the motor cortex result in impaired movement or paralysis of corresponding body parts. In now classic electrical stimulation studies, performed by Canadian neurosurgeon Wilder Penfield, it was revealed that the motor cortex is somatotopically organized, with more expansive representations for body parts that require fine motor control, such as the hands and face.

This might work in text, but when speaking, you'd be far better off with a version containing less jargon:

The motor cortex sits just in front of the central sulcus and is crucial for voluntary movement. We know this because damage to the motor cortex impairs movement. It was a Canadian neurosurgeon called Wilder Penfield who showed that the motor cortex contains a map of the body, with larger parts of the map controlling body parts that need fine control, like the hands and the face.

If you're losing people with language that is too flowery, you will not achieve your goal of making sure everyone gets it.

When explaining methods, consider using diagrams of the experimental design and protocol if appropriate. A very important component of presenting research papers is the results section. When you present the results from the paper, whatever you do, do not skip over graphs quickly, and always, always make sure the axes on any graphs are clearly labelled, with units indicated (for example, "reaction time (milliseconds)"). Take the time to explain what the x-axis and y-axis represent and what the graph shows. Point to bars or data points while you speak and ask people if what you've said is clear. Remember not to spend the whole time looking at the screen when you do this. A simple glance while you point to a noteworthy result is fine. Offer to re-explain the graph if you have a feeling that anyone in the room didn't get it. Better still, explain it twice anyway but using different words. This is useful because no one usually gets it the first time! Explaining results twice also demonstrates to the professor that you are so confident in your understanding of the material that you are prepared to

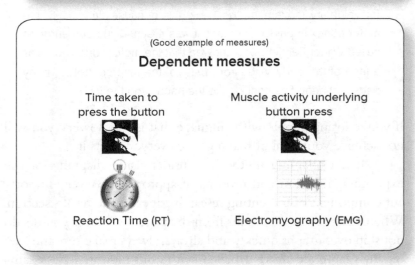

Figure 2.3 Bad and Good Experiment Measures Slides

explain the results in different ways to help people understand. Don't present all the statistics; if something is significantly different from something else, say so, and perhaps indicate a p-value on the graph, but don't put the full extent of the statistical result on slides. This comes down to having an understanding of what is important information and what is detail that you can do without in a time-limited presentation. Skilfully making these judgments between details and essential content is the sign of an A+ student!

(Basic ending slide, acceptable but not very engaging)

Take-home message

- In order to end the unnecessary deaths
- Need to work on:
  - Systems to weed out "bad apples"
  - Subculture that focuses on violence and crime
  - Improving organizational elements to allow for better supervision and better training on the use of force

(Good, hard-hitting, and engaging ending slide)

Take-home message

(Good, hard-hitting and engaging ending slide, animates to this)

Take home message

- Identify and filter out "bad apples"
- Change police "subculture"
- Change organizational structure

Figure 2.4   Bad and Good Ending Slides

However, you obviously cannot do this if you have not put the time and effort into preparing.

A Strong Ending

Your ending, just like your beginning, should be solid. This is where you get to reveal the take-home message of your talk—this is what you've been building up to all along. Be concise but be extremely clear in how you articulate the take-home message. Usually, for a common research paper with all the normal sections going from introduction to conclusion, you can do a quick summary on the penultimate (or next-to-last) slide to highlight what the paper is about and what your substantive critical thoughts are (along with a couple of outstanding questions), before presenting your final take-home. I am a fan of making the final statement memorable and well justified. Make sure the ending makes sense given your goal for the talk, which you may have shared with your audience at the beginning. Whatever happens, your conclusion should not sound as if it came out of nowhere; you should have been building up to it throughout your talk and it should make sense given the opening remarks and your goal for the talk. Often a graphic slide is a nice way to end, or if you must use a bulleted list, use no more than three single-line bullet points. You should try to ensure that your final slide stays up for as long as possible to give people the chance to fully take in your conclusion. Finally, after your concluding remarks, it is customary to have a "final final" slide saying something like "Thanks for listening," or "Questions?".

Mind Mapping for Success

When it comes to putting ideas together and being able to see an overview of a topic or how you might explain a topic with reference to important concepts and ideas, mind mapping is a great tool. There are many mind mapping programs on the market nowadays, or you can use the old-school pen and paper approach. The basic idea with mind mapping is to start with a central concept or topic and then draw branches connecting other related concepts. For example, you can have five main branches that emerge from a central topic and then have five sub-branches for each of the five main branches. While simple pencil and paper planning is also perfectly useful, it never hurts to look at the newer tools that are out there, in the form of apps for example, to help you lay out your thoughts. One particularly good piece of software for mind mapping is iMindMap by ThinkBuzan, which is available to download and purchase at www.thinkbuzan.com. There are also an array of free options including the open-source mind mapping app called xMind and one of my personal favourites, Coggle, which can be accessed using your Google account login and password. Check out Coggle at www.coggle.it. An example mind map for a presentation is shown in Figure 2.5.

Designing the Presentation

Remember, the point of presenting a research paper is to "explain" the paper to the class and the professor and to provide some critical analysis. Over the years, I have identified a number of things that I think virtually always improve a presentation in a class setting:

1. Have a goal and consider revealing this goal to your audience at the start of your talk; reference it again when wrapping up.
2. Keep it simple and do not fall into the trap of using jargon or technical language unless it is absolutely necessary.
3. Tell a story, and make it easy to digest for the audience.
4. Think about the background knowledge that people in the audience have.
5. Pitch the presentation to maximize the chances that everyone in the room will understand.
6. Use other papers to provide background or supporting information.

Have a goal. It's always a good idea to have a goal in mind for what you want people to take away. Sometimes I've seen speakers explicitly state what they want people to take away at the end of the presentation. For example, if your topic is "police brutality," you might say something like, "By the end of this presentation, I hope to have convinced you that police brutality is a serious and com-

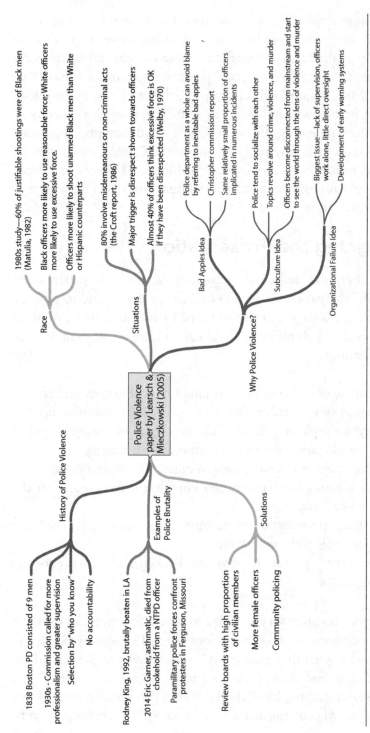

Figure 2.5 A Mind Map of a Presentation on Police Violence That Might Be Part of a Sociology Seminar

mon problem in our cities and that an overhaul of the regulatory framework within which police services operate is in order."

Keep it simple. Using overly technical terms and lots of jargon doesn't make you look smart. Try to break the concepts under consideration into simple descriptions and use specialized language only when you are sure that everyone in the room will understand what you're talking about.

Tell a story. One thing I recommend, before you start putting slides together, is to come up with at least *two* ways you *could* present the paper. What is the story? Is it best to explain it one way, or another? For example, does one way afford the use of analogies or metaphors that could be employed to get key concepts across? Research indicates that analogies and metaphors can help with retention of presented material (Garner, 2005). These approaches work by associating concepts that may be unfamiliar with concepts that are already known. In psychology, one of the most famous metaphors is the computer metaphor that likens human thinking to information processing by a computer—a process that has inputs, operations, and outputs. Studies have shown that the use of metaphors in teaching improves the ability to make inferences relating to the material and aids answering problems about the material (Evans, 1988).

In addition to the use of analogies and metaphors, you might want to think about whether one approach offers the chance to use humour to a greater extent that another approach. Humour has been shown to create a more comfortable classroom environment, and relevant humour can facilitate recognition memory for information (Garner, 2005; Suzuki & Heath, 2014). Be careful though, you should not come across as a stand-up comedian and if the class you're in is multicultural, some students or even the professor may not appreciate your jokes (Wang, 2014). Finally, you might ask why I recommend thinking of two ways to present a paper. Well, thinking of more than one way to present the paper is useful because it helps avoid the temptation to just go with whatever comes to mind initially. It's important to take the time to consider alternative ways of telling a story, with thought given to who you are talking to. The best way to pitch things may not be the way *you* find easiest to follow. An extreme example of this is if you had to explain the concept of money to a group of kindergarten kids, you would have to think hard about what pre-existing knowledge you could and could not assume.

Think about background knowledge and pitch appropriately. The first thing about explaining something to someone is to make sure you are speaking in a language they understand. So, if the paper has a lot of jargon, an attempt should be made to explain what the jargon means. I always tell my students to imagine that the audience is made up of intelligent high school students. If you can figure out a way to explain the paper to a group like this, you will succeed in the goal of making sure everyone in the room gets it. In a review of effective teaching strategies, Feldman (1989) found that *clarity and understandability* and *organization and preparedness* were the most important teaching characteristics as identified by both students and teachers. Following these characteristics, *stimulation of interest* emerged as one of the next most important characteristics. There is no single recipe for stimulation of interest, but by thinking about the people in the room and tailoring your approach to what you think will engage them, you give yourself a much better chance at doing well than if you don't consider this. I urge you to consider again what I said about taking into account the "who" question. It's absolutely vital to delivering an appropriate presentation.

Reference other papers. This is a simple way to get across to your professor that you've gone beyond the main paper and have researched the broader topic. This cannot fail to help bump your grade! Make sure to say something along the lines of, "I spent some time digging around the literature and came up with an interesting find…." Basically, I advocate telling your professor and the class that you did this "extra" work.

Putting the Slides Together

Choose what you think is the best of the two ways you have come up with, and start creating PowerPoint slides with bulleted text. Don't worry, the slides will not remain as bulleted text, but you can start this way. When you do this, you need to be fully cognizant of the time constraints for the presentation. Try to think logically through the explanation process. How will you build the story of the paper? At this stage your slides can be thought of as a storyboard for your presentation. Don't limit the number of slides you create on this first pass. Trimming, being more selective, and general re-jigging will come later. In general, the order of sections in a research paper presentation should include the sections illustrated below (or a similar kind of structure):

1. Title slide
2. Background/contextualization slide
3. Clear statement of the research question and hypotheses
4. Approach/method including the experimental design if appropriate
5. Results
6. Interpretation/what does it mean?
7. Evaluation of the work—what do you think they did well and not so well?
8. Summary of the whole thing

Within this general framework, there is much room for making the content and style uniquely yours. Although in the list above I've indicated that you might evaluate the work at the end of the presentation, consider providing critical thoughts *during* the presentation as well (but not at the cost of flow), or at least making people aware that you have a critical thought about a specific component of the work and will discuss it later. Once you have put all the slides together, try going through them and thinking about what you will say on each slide, and roughly how long it will take you to say it. As you go through the presentation for the first time, continue to ask yourself whether the flow is good, or whether it could be improved. I find that it is usually impossible to make decisions about the flow of a presentation until a set of slides is prepared and you try to talk through them. At this stage, you will often move from one slide to the next and realize that the way you thought you would explain it doesn't flow well, or doesn't make sense. As you go through your first set of bulleted text slides, work diligently on the issue of flow—you are essentially shaping your storyboard into the best flowing story possible. This is an iterative process and may take some time. Slide titles can often help with flow. If you think about the presentation as a story, each slide title should make sense in the context of the previous one. During this whole process you should also have been thinking about time constraints and making sure that your timing is in the ball park of what's required.

Making the Slides Awesome

There are a number of general considerations when you start thinking about making slides for a presentation. In a very recent paper, Kosslyn et al. (2012) outlined eight cognitive principles that can usefully be borne in mind when designing PowerPoint slides. These authors did a *task analysis* of psychological processes involved when following a PowerPoint presentation and came up with eight important principles based on the extant psychology literature. Using these principles as a guide, I recommend thinking about the following points when designing slides:

1. Important information has to be readily distinguishable from not-so-important information. Make sure important information is easily visible from every part of the room. Text size is an important consideration here as is background colour and pattern. In general, keep backgrounds simple and avoid the use of overly artistic themes. If possible, you should test out a sample text size in the actual room you'll be presenting in and make sure it is clearly visible from all parts of the room. My strong recommendation is to use light or dark backgrounds with dark or light text, and avoid the use of backgrounds with designs on them. They may look nice, but they also provide yet another element for people to attend to and thus are potentially distracting. White or yellow text on a black or dark grey background works well, as does dark text (black, dark grey) on a light background. Avoid using red and green for text or for adjacent elements as distinguishing between these colours is often impaired in individuals who are colour blind. Similarly, individuals cannot focus well on red and blue at the same time, so don't present these colours adjacent to one another.

2. The brain tends to perceive multiple elements as grouped under certain conditions. Specific conditions have been identified by psychologists and are referred to "gestalt" principles. "Gestalt" literally means "an organized whole that is greater than the sum of its parts." Consider using **common colour to group certain elements** and make them distinct from others. You can also use proximity to group elements together (e.g., JJJ JJJ is seen as two groups of three Js and not six individual Js). Headings are usually interpreted as referring to the closest image or diagram. Only use different colours to differentiate things you want to be seen as distinct—don't just use colours as "art." You can also group elements **by using a common font** such as I just did. However, too many colours or too many fonts produce too many perceptual groups and can be overwhelming, so keep the number of different colours and fonts used under five, if possible.

3. People are more likely to notice something when it is different from the background or stimuli surrounding it, that is, when it is salient. A moving stimulus is salient when presented within other stationary elements. Motion captures attention. However, as mentioned earlier, from my poll of social science professors, animations don't seem to be very highly weighted as necessary components of a great presentation. This doesn't mean that you shouldn't use them, only that you should use them intelligently and not gratuitously. One method for making your picture or text stand out is to fade out other elements on the slide. This has the effect of increasing the salience of the non-faded out information—effectively bringing it to the foreground, which in turn makes it easier for the audience to attend to the message you are trying to get across.

4. People have limited capacity to process information and can generally only hold about four perceptual groups in mind at any one time, so don't overcrowd slides. By reducing the clutter on slides you also make it easier for the attentional system to extract the relevant information. There are ways to make sure information is displayed in a way that minimizes strain on capacity, for example, using direct labelling instead of keys on figures. Processing limitations can also be overcome by

providing more time for people to take in information. This is why it is critical to keep figures and graphs up on the screen for ample time for people to process them.

5. Changes in the display should be informative and not arbitrary. Breaking your presentation into sections and clearly marking the beginning and end of each section with some discernible changes helps make the information you're trying to get across more digestible. It also helps people remember the information (i.e., by presenting important information at the beginning and end of sections—the primacy and recency effects). As mentioned above, intelligent use of animations can help in building up a complex figure or set of ideas. Flying in key ideas or elements helps direct attention to the incoming points and can be effective. Again though, animations have to be meaningful. Too much arbitrary animation is distracting and can be annoying!

6. The way you tell the story of the paper should be appropriate. This relates to the idea of knowing your audience that was mentioned earlier. When information is presented, people make sense of it by forming connections with information they already have stored in long-term memory (Reisberg, 2005). This is the reason why analogies are useful; you use them to help people connect new information to already stored information. In this way, new information is more readily integrated into the knowledge networks of the brain. So again, think about the background knowledge held by your audience and use an appropriate strategy.

7. Compatibility between the physical appearance of an element and the meaning of the element helps understanding. You wouldn't explain what Arial font is by writing in Times New Roman. Rather, **Arial font would be much more compatible and help your audience absorb the information.** Likewise you wouldn't present information that "cats are generally smaller than dogs" like this.

In addition to these key recommendations, there are also other things to think about such as including slide numbers so that audience members can easily reference your slides when making notes or asking questions. Some people make a big deal out of using serif fonts such as Times New Roman or sans serif fonts such as Arial. My preference has always been to use sans serif fonts to improve clarity, but there is no reason why you shouldn't use serif fonts if you've tested for discriminability and visibility and the slides look good. It is important however not to flip from one font to another for no good reason. Unless explicitly asked for, I am not a fan of using handouts unless there is a reason for students to take the information presented and use it for another activity at a later time. Handouts can actually distract people away from you and your verbal delivery, thus dividing an already stressed cognitive capacity even further. If you are specifically walking people through the handout, that could work, but for class presentations, I generally advise students not to make handouts. Finally, it is very important to test your potential colour scheme in the room you are going to present in, if at all possible. Even with multiple recommendations and guidelines, one of the best ways of ensuring that your slides are clear and compelling is to test them on site. It is not always possible to get to the room, so if this is the case, you should err on the side of caution and design slides so that they are likely to be easily visible by a majority of people without too much effort. At a minimum, this means keeping text and images distinct from the background, and making sure text size is large enough to be seen from the other side of the room.

Reducing Text Is Important

With these general tips in mind, let's think about reducing text and increasing the use of diagrams and pictures. Figure 2.6 provides an example of converting a textual slide into more of a pictorial slide that you can talk through. This is the part of preparing a presentation that I really enjoy. It is also a hard part because it is not always obvious how five bulleted points in text can be converted to a pictorial depiction. Minimizing text is a key thing that I *strongly recommend*. Research has confirmed that concurrent presentation of aural and textual linguistic stimuli creates cognitive load that impairs the uptake of information (Mayer, 2001). This is a case of a dual task (trying to do two things at the same time). When the two tasks use similar

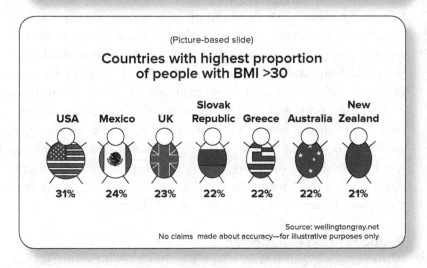

Figure 2.6 Text-Based Slide to Picture-Based Slide

cognitive processes, interference occurs which makes it hard to attend to the information being presented. On the other hand, if the two tasks require different processes, it is easier to attend to the message. This is the reason why trying to learn textual material while listening to a radio talk show is harder than learning the same material while listening to instrumental music. I would bet that most professors who grade presentations for a living will agree that less text results in a better presentation, all other things being equal. So, after you have slides that you think flow well, I recommend that you go through each and every slide and ask yourself the following question: "How can I change this text to a picture or diagram, or at least, how can I reduce the amount of text?" Using pictures and diagrams also makes presentations more interesting and more readily serves to *supplement and not duplicate* what you are saying. Note, though, that I'm not advocating that you totally eliminate text—it is completely permissible to use minimal text in the form of well-placed words or bulleted points that can help orient people to your message. What I am saying is try not to rely on text where a picture could have been effective. Finally, pictures and diagrams are important because they help make sure you understand what you need to say. With pictures and diagrams, there is no option to just read the bullet points; you have to know your stuff to be able to talk people through pictures or diagrams.

Top Tip

A good strategy that will impress your professor is to use predominantly pictures and diagrams on your slides with text only for slide titles and labels and succinct bullet points to help reinforce key take-home points. Your professor will be able to see that you're not just reading off the slides and that you must have put a lot of work into understanding the material. Of course, if you haven't done your preparation, this approach can also lead to a crash-and-burn situation! So, bear in mind, simply using lots of pictures is not a magic trick to earn you a better grade; you still have to *deliver* the presentation!

A Note on Presenting the Results Section of a Paper

An important part of a research paper presentation is the results section. You should think carefully about the best way to present the data from the paper. Should you cut and paste graphs from the PDF file? Or should you create your own graphs that show the results in an easier to explain or digest manner? If you choose to do the latter, make sure you make a statement in the seminar something like: "The graphs that the authors put in the paper were quite confusing, so to make it easier to follow, I took the liberty of re-presenting the data in the following way..." This looks amazing to a professor. A student who has gone to the trouble of realizing that the original graphs are not the best way to get the point across and who has done some work to re-present the graphs differently is well on their way to getting a better grade!

In addition, be cognizant that different types of graphs lend themselves to the presentation of different types of information. For example, if you're presenting data collected over time, you may find it better to use a line graph to show a trend, as opposed to multiple bar graphs. Similarly, if you're presenting data about groups or conditions (on the horizontal axis), a bar graph may be better. In experiments where interactions are present in the results, it is often clearer to use line graphs to depict them. If at all possible, I'd avoid presenting tables in slide shows. If you really must use tables, make sure you plan to leave the slide up for long enough to allow the audience to process the data. Alternatively, you could choose to present a complex table from the paper and use it to reinforce the fact that you've *re-presented* the data by saying something like, "The authors presented their results in this table, which I'm sure you'd all agree is very difficult to decipher. I've plotted out the important results to make it easier to extract the main findings." All in all, you should be thinking about the clearest way to present data and not necessarily the most complex or clever-looking way. Clarity always trumps complexity when it comes to presentations.

Finishing Touches

Now that you have an amazing set of slides, it is time to re-think whether all your slides are needed or whether you need to get rid of some (or even add some). Often you can only determine this after you've practiced the talk for the first time to see if it really flows as well as you thought it would. In general, have an appropriate number of slides so that you can spend at least one or two minutes per slide on average. Anything less than this just looks like you're flipping through slides to create an animation! This means, for a 20-minute presentation, 10 to 20 slides are permissible. However, I would only approach the upper limit of 20 if there is no more efficient way to get all the material across. Finally, use presenter's notes in PowerPoint to provide cues for what you are saying on each slide. Do not write a speech in presenter's notes. It never comes across well, and is easy to spot as reading. Presenter's notes are a great tool in PowerPoint if you have done your preparation and the notes simply serve as cues for the points you need to make. Ideally though, you should be able to give your presentation without notes or cue cards of any kind.

Practice, Practice, Practice . . . and Practice Some More!

When you have got to the point of having a beautiful set of slides that you think flow well, your job is to practice, practice some more, and practice some more. I usually find that, by the third time going through a presentation, it starts to get good. People often believe that they can "wing it" on the day as long as they know their stuff. Unfortunately, it's not usually that easy. Even if you are smart and know the material, unless you've practiced what you are going to say on each slide, you are likely to screw up, or at least have to pause, and maybe mutter to yourself. I once attended a lecture by a very famous neuroscientist. He was clearly using a slide deck from a previous talk and had not bothered to tailor the presentation for the crowd he was now in front of. In a word, the presentation was awful. He flipped through several slides without talking about them and stumbled a few times because he had forgotten what he was going to emphasize. Frankly, he messed up, and he was a seasoned pro! So, take it from me, practice is essential for delivering a clear talk and thus getting a great grade; do not try to wing it if you are serious about doing well. Here are 10 critical things to bear in mind as you practice your presentation:

1. Where will you stand when you present, and how will you ensure an engaging start in which you emphasize your goal for the talk? Will you be able to refer to your presenter's notes?
2. Keep timing in mind, and even keep a timer or watch in sight so you know whether you're where you need to be to finish on time.

3. Make sure you look at the audience and not at the screen—although glancing at the screen when explaining certain details is fine. Don't talk to the screen all the way through the presentation!
4. Talk S L O W L Y—in fact, you cannot talk too slowly! When you are nervous on the day, there will be a tendency to talk quickly. Be cognizant of this and practice speaking slowly and deliberately. (As a useful exercise, focus on how slowly news reporters talk next time you watch a news show on television.)
5. Repeat key concepts, perhaps by paraphrasing (using different words to say the same thing).
6. Ask for feedback—questions such as, "Is that clear to everyone?" or "I can say that again if it's unclear," show that you are thinking about clarity and create a good impression with professors. Even if people act as if they understand what you've said, repeat key points anyway—remember you want to require the least work from your audience.
7. Give interim summaries at the end of sections, to help audience members extract the main idea(s).
8. Don't be monotone—be upbeat and lively if possible, but too many jokes and too much informality or gesturing might detract from your presentation and possibly be annoying.
9. Regarding point 8 above, take cues about style from the way your professor acts. Have they got a sense of humour? Do they make jokes when they present? Try to align a little with their style. Everyone has unconscious biases, and this is a trick that can help bump your mark!
10. This is fundamental: does your ending refer back to the goal you outlined (or the goal you had in mind) at the beginning and does it "end the story" well?

Bearing this list of 10 things in mind will help you pitch your presentation in the best possible way. Once you've practiced the presentation to yourself a few times, try it out on some friends or family and make sure they get what you're trying to say. Often, presenting to a non-specialist audience can help you spot things that you had taken for granted or that you could explain more clearly.

Finally, take a positive attitude toward presentations. See presentations as opportunities to showcase the knowledge you've amassed about your topic and appreciate the valuable experience you're getting with an important real-world skill. If you have a positive attitude about your own presentation, the audience will follow your lead, and the chances that you will be positively evaluated will increase.

Recommended Further Reading

Kosslyn, S. (2007). *Clear and to the point.* New York, NY: Oxford University Press.

Schultz, S. (2009). *Eloquent science: A practical guide to becoming a better writer, speaker and atmospheric scientist.* Boston, MA: American Meteorological Society.

Reynolds. G. (2012). *Presentation Zen: Simple ideas on presentation design and delivery* (2nd ed.). Berkeley, CA: New Riders.

3
Delivering Presentations

If I Had a Penny for Every "I'm Sick" Email I've Received on Presentation Day . . . I'd Be Rich!

It's funny how sickness strikes and sports accidents happen the night before presentations! If only I could show you the number of student emails I've received over the years either the night before or the morning of a presentation. You'd be surprised (or maybe you wouldn't). I've even had students drop my course a few days before their presentation was due. All of this points to the fact that many students find the lead-up to and the day of the presentation stressful. Rather than diminish this point, let me say that even professors and other people who speak for a living find presentation days somewhat stressful. Arguably, the key goal should be to work with stress and indeed, make stress work for you, rather than try to eliminate it. Unfortunately, presentations are such that *execution matters*. The best preparation in the world will not get you that great mark you so desperately want if you fail to execute. This is analogous to saying that you won't get credit for studying really hard for an exam if during the exam you circle answer "d" for every question. Rest assured, I'm not saying this to stress you out even more, but to help bring into awareness the reality that all the preparation you'll do prior to a presentation is *for* something, and that thing is to knock it out of the park (or close) on the day! Whenever performance is critical, anxiety and worry will rear their heads and try to wreak havoc. This, it seems, is human nature and I don't know many people who are immune. In fact, the few people I have met who are not fazed by having to perform usually have not given good performances—which is clearly not what you want, otherwise you wouldn't be reading this guide. Much of this chapter will be devoted to thinking about optimizing your ability to do well on the day, but I'll also point out that doing worse than you wanted or even "bombing" it completely (whatever that constitutes in your opinion) are both not as bad as your anxious mind might think. Lastly, given that preparing a presentation and actually giving it are so intertwined, this chapter covers some things that could equally have been included in the last chapter. So, my best advice is to see this and the previous chapter as a package deal.

Remember Your Goal for the Talk

I mentioned in the previous chapter that you should have a goal for your presentation. It's up to you whether you choose to share the goal with the audience or not, but a goal helps to focus the process as a means to an end—with the end being some change in the minds of the people listening to you. What do I mean by this exactly? Well, when someone is exposed to ideas, these ideas connect with the knowledge they have in long-term memory and, if retained, these ideas *change* the web of knowledge in their brain. This brain "plasticity" results in relatively long-term changes to neural networks that code knowledge and is what constitutes learning. When giving a talk, then, set yourself an objective for how you want people to be affected by your talk. When they walk out of the room after your talk, how do you want them to be different from when they walked in? Asking yourself this question will help you figure out the whole point of your presentation. Remembering this goal on presentation day helps to re-focus you on the job at hand.

As alluded to in the previous chapter, you're going for a strong beginning, a compelling middle, and a memorable, clear, and reinforcing ending. These are the components you should emphasize as you move through your talk. As also mentioned in the previous chapter—speak slowly and clearly and keep an eye on the time.

A Note on Starting

Arguably the hardest part of doing a presentation is the start, not least because as you sit there waiting for your turn or as you walk to class knowing you'll be the first to present, you're probably nervous, playing your presentation through in your mind. Although I'll talk more about dealing with nerves later, the ability to re-focus yourself as you start to feel nervous is highly relevant for the few minutes *just before* you present. If you find yourself feeling anxious, take some deep breaths and then visualize yourself making an excellent start—the one you have practiced numerous times. If you can make sure you execute the start well, the rest will often follow. Once you get into your stride, your preparation kicks in and as long as you've prepared meticulously, things will fall into place. Speaking of interesting and compelling starts, once, at a conference, I was drifting off at the back of the room while sitting through a series of boring presentations. While I was in that semi-awake mode, a new speaker went up to start his talk which was going to be on spatial attention. I was on the verge of dropping off but this guy started his talk by almost shouting something like: "Hey, what would happen if I threw a brick through that window?" (while he pointed to a large floor-to-ceiling window to his left). I can honestly say that after this opening, I was wide awake. I wanted to hear what he was going to say next. The general rule of a good opening is to get people to want to listen.

One thing you should never do at the start is begin with an apology or an admission of being nervous. I have seen many students start this way by saying something like, "Sorry, I'm really nervous, so please bear with me." I wouldn't recommend this; it doesn't work and it looks bad. Much better to focus and crack on with the task in the best way you can. People are generally sympathetic, especially because they know they'll be up in front of the class soon enough; you already have their sympathy. Asking for it explicitly is totally unnecessary. Finally, an outline slide is sometimes a good idea but should not precede your attention-grabbing opening slide, and in many cases can be omitted all together.

Top Tip
Your opening remarks should be attention grabbing and should motivate the audience to want to hear what you'll say next. Obviously, you can't be inappropriate (this would also grab attention), so you need to think this through carefully during preparation.

Presentation Style

Be You!
You are an individual with your own personality and characteristic way of speaking. Never be afraid to use this, unless *everyone you've ever known* has told you your way of speaking is rude, condescending, or otherwise irritating and annoying! If this is you, some reflection, personal development, and remediation might be something to consider. In reality, though, this is exceedingly rare. Even the most obnoxious people are not obnoxious *all* the time! In general then, play to your personality and style, not against it. One aspect of style is dress. Students often ask if they should dress a certain way when presenting. Answers to this might vary by professor, but I usually don't put any constraints on what students wear when presenting. If you feel that dressing a certain way helps you perform your best, go for it. On the same note, if you feel that dress has no bearing on how well you present, forget about it! In that informal poll of social science professors that I mentioned in the last chapter, the issue of what students wear when presenting was ranked as being the least important of a number of other criteria. So don't sweat it. You should however, use common sense; it's probably not a great idea to dress like you're going clubbing or for a swim, and probably best to make sure your fly is done up and your shoelaces are tied. Beyond this, don't stress about attire. Clothes though, are only one aspect of how you present yourself. Demeanour is also key. As mentioned in the previous chapter, if

you're using humour, be appropriate and relevant. Telling a joke about this drunk guy you saw puking at a house party might help break the ice, but probably doesn't qualify as relevant or appropriate, unless your presentation is on drinking habits of university students. Likewise, being overly serious and rigid, if that's not your natural style, is probably not a great idea either. Most people respond well to genuine and sincere individuals. Keeping this in mind is probably a good idea. Think about it.

In general, it's helpful to speak slowly and clearly and repeat key concepts. Don't walk around too much as this can be distracting, but try not to stand rigidly still throughout the presentation either (some walking is fine!).

Body Language

Body language and eye contact are very important communicative tools. In terms of body language, posture especially conveys a lot of information. In general, an open body posture, forward leaning or stepping toward the audience, nodding, and smiling convey an engaging, positive, non-dominant orientation, whereas a closed body posture, backward leaning or stepping back or turning away from the audience, and a knitted brow convey dominance, a lack of engagement, and emotional distance (Burgoon, 1990; Mehrabian & Williams, 1969). This is all very well, but you might ask, what exactly does an open and closed body posture constitute? Well, open body postures are basically postures where your arms are at your side or extended away from your body midline, and your palms are open. In contrast, closed body postures involve crossed arms, elbows held very close to the body, hands clasped, and so on. The difference between how people evaluate other individuals on the basis of body posture alone is quite striking. In an early study, McGinley et al. (1978) found that individuals who display an open posture while addressing another individual are evaluated more positively than those who display a closed posture. One important thing for presenters to appreciate is that turning away from your audience, whether during your actual presentation, or perhaps when someone asks a question, is not good for interpersonal smoothness and can create the impressions that you are uninterested and avoidant—turning even 45 degrees away reduces engagement (Matsumoto & Sung Hwang, 2013). When speaking, adopting an open symmetrical posture (both arms to the side) signals higher rapport than an asymmetrical posture (for example, one arm by your side and the other leaning on a desk). As well as being conscious about your own posture, it is important to look for cues in the audience too. When people lean toward you, it can convey that they are very interested in what you are saying. Use this body language cue as a means to pick someone to engage with for a moment. These tips all help in allowing you to negotiate the presentation time effectively and in an engaging manner.

Of course, posture is not the only form of body language that is important. Hand gesturing is also a common occurrence in any form of communicative engagement. There are two main types of hand gesture: so-called speech illustrators and emblems. Speech illustrators, as the name suggests, are the kinds of hand movements that are tied to speech and help illustrate what you are saying. For example, you might use your hands to represent events that unfold over time by making one hand movement followed by another one a slight horizontal distance away. If you're presenting a paper about the likelihood of men and women being stopped by traffic police, you might first ask your audience to guess which gender gets stopped the most. Assuming an audience member answers the question and suggests that women gets stopped more than men, you might hold your hands at different vertical heights to illustrate their guess (as if to signify two different heights of bars on hypothetical bar graph). When you present the actual statistic from your paper which actually shows no difference, you might use both hands now placed at the same vertical height to illustrate this (as if you're indicating the height of two equal bars on a graph). Pointing is also a form of speech illustrator. In short, most of us use speech illustrators all the time without thinking—indeed, these kinds of gestures are largely held to be unconsciously initiated (Matsumoto & Sung Hwang, 2013). The second kind of gesture, speech emblems constitute things like a thumbs up, and an A-okay sign (index finger and thumb touching with other fingers extended). Gesturing in general is thought to lighten cognitive load while someone is figuring out what to say. When individuals are asked to memorize some information while explaining how to solve a math problem, they remember more if they gesture during the explanation (Goldin-Meadow et al., 2001). Interestingly, and perhaps useful to know, gesturing has even been shown to help children learn—that is, when the children themselves gesture during learning, they learn more effectively than when they don't (Wagner Cook et al., 2008). One application of this could be that during your reading of the paper, when "explaining" the paper to yourself, gestures may help you remember the material better. Finally, in one study, instructors with a relaxed posture, who smiled, and who were vocally expressive created more positive affect in students (Anderson & Anderson, 1987). In summary, gestures can help to explain concepts during speech, but perhaps more importantly, research shows that gesturing helps the speaker by reducing cognitive load. This potentially leaves more capacity for other cognitive processes like retrieving information from memory (Goldin-Meadow, 1999).

Top Tip

In general, try to adopt an open body posture when talking and avoid body language that distances you from your audience. Be aware of gesturing, and play to your natural style, but if you are a "hand-talker" be careful not to flail around as this might be distracting. You should make an effort to think about how gesturing might play a role in how you communicate certain concepts in your talk. Also, gesturing can help you, the speaker, by reducing cognitive load.

Eye Contact

Eye contact is obviously crucial for effective presenting. Pretty much all my students raise this as a really important thing that improves presentations when I ask them what they think constitutes a great presentation. They are not wrong! Studies show that people who make more eye contact are judged as more sociable and competent and even more truthful and credible (see, for example, Beebe, 1974; Cook, 1977). We also know that during listening, people engage in higher levels of eye contact than during speaking, so when you're presenting, be aware that many people are trying to engage with you through eye contact. It never looks great when a student spends all their time looking at the floor or staring at the screen. In fact, research shows a lack of eye contact leads to being interpreted as nervous and low in self-confidence and these are things you want to avoid (Cook & Smith, 1975). Try to engage with people in the audience, especially by feeding off their eye contact toward you. Oftentimes you will notice that one or two people in particular seem to be paying a lot of attention to what you're saying. Feed off these people and direct your gaze toward them preferentially, while also looking around at others from time to time. Take care to look at the professor as well, as they will want to feel that you are trying to engage with them. This again is a sign of a great student and a great presenter.

In addition to its positive utility, eye contact can also be a point of frustration during communication. For example, if there's a particularly difficult question or tense debate about an issue (which can sometimes happen in the discussion period after a presentation), a longish gaze becomes a stare that can make people feel uncomfortable. In some contexts (in non-human and human groups), staring is an aggressive signal (think of two mixed martial arts fighters staring each other down at a pre-fight weigh-in). Cultural differences also exist in the way that eye contact is perceived. For example, Americans tend to make more eye contact than those from Asian cultures, which sometimes can produce discomfort in multicultural settings. In contrast, people from Arabic countries tend to make more eye contact than Americans, so again,

Top Tip

Eye contact is one of your most powerful tools for engaging with your audience. However, try to make contact with people around the room, by feeding off their eye contact and body language cues. In my lectures, I sometimes focus in on students who are maintaining gaze, nodding, and leaning forward. In a normal class, I can usually identify several such students around the room and by switching between them, I can increase the chances that I am seen to be addressing the whole audience. You may want to try this approach.

the discordance in what is "normal" can cause frustration. These are things to be aware of if your group is made up of people from multiple cultures.

Get Inspired

This tip could have gone into the preparation chapter, but I'll put it here while we're talking about presenting with style. You might know that before a game, many top athletes spend time watching sports videos, perhaps of themselves performing in a previous game or of other athletes who inspire them. This helps prime them for the ensuing game and can be a great motivator for performing well. When it comes to giving talks and thinking about style and other aspects of presentations, YouTube can be an amazing tool. With the thousands of talks and lectures available on YouTube you could literally spend days watching some of the world's best presenters give talks. Whether it's a TED talk or a freely available lecture from an Ivy League professor, you have an unprecedented opportunity to trawl the internet for examples of good presentation skills. As you watch, think about their presentation style. What is it that makes them so compelling? What's their body language like? How do they build the story of the talk they are giving? Students today are extremely lucky to have these types of resources available online—use them. If you have a favourite presenter, think about trying to emulate their style, as long as it isn't totally incompatible with your own personal style. Have fun doing this online research; it's educational and enjoyable.

Coping with Nerves

Almost every person feels nerves of some kind when faced with a situation in which they will be evaluated. For many, these nerves may take the form of butterflies in the stomach, increased heart rate, sweating, a dry mouth, and possibly even light-headedness. These are indices of arousal and typical components of an anxiety response. If this describes the way you feel prior to giving a presentation in a seminar or other venue, please know that you are *not* alone. Many, many people, including very successful public speakers, experience these symptoms when preparing for and giving a presentation. For many students, presenting in a seminar or tutorial class is their first experience of speaking to a group, and especially of speaking to a professor. While many students overcome their nerves very well, for some, nerves can be debilitating. In fact, some students are so scared by the prospect of giving a presentation that they will avoid classes with a presentation component altogether. This is a shame, as seminar and tutorial environments should be viewed as a supportive opportunity to develop useful oral presentation skills that will serve you well, no matter what field you end up working in.

Psychologists refer to a situation in which performance will be evaluated as an "achievement situation." A person's achievement motivation is their propensity to approach or avoid an achievement situation and is believed to be produced by the motivation to achieve success balanced against the fear of failure. Without going into details, if an individual's self-confidence with a task is stronger than their fear of failing at the task, they will approach the achievement situation. The fact that you are registered for a seminar course is proof that your self-confidence to do what is required is stronger than your fear of failing. This is something you should feel good about! Even though you might be apprehensive about some components of the course, try to see these as learning experiences that will only make you a better all-round individual.

Luckily, although being evaluated can produce a great deal of nerves, there are concrete steps that can be taken to turn a potentially negative, anxiety-producing experience into one you look forward to and eventually (after much practice and some successes) relish. Again, a seminar or tutorial at the undergraduate level should be viewed as a supportive environment in which to hone skills that are essential to many jobs and professions. Therefore, at least some of the responsibility for creating this environment should fall on the professor. Usually, professors are very supportive and understand that students can find presentations challenging and nerve-racking. Undoubtedly, there are also professors who are not so supportive, focusing only on the outcome and not the process of helping students achieve their best. Unfortunately, as a student, you have very little control over the disposition of your professor, so it's best not to rely on them, but rather take the necessary steps to maximize your chances of success.

I recommend a five-point plan for dealing with and overcoming nerves in the seminar environment:

1. Think through the seminar situation: What are you here to learn? What are your fears? What skills do you want to improve?
2. Have a contingency plan, especially for the "no-slides" scenario (see below), and use structured visualization for all eventualities.
3. Use self-talk to cognitively re-interpret bodily symptoms of nerves.
4. Focus on what you must do, not what you must not do.
5. Practice, practice, and practice some more.

Sports and performance psychologists have come up with a variety of tools and approaches for helping athletes and performers cope with anxiety and nerves prior to competition. Although a seminar presentation is not a competition, it is undoubtedly an achievement situation. From my own experience in doing quite a bit of speaking and watching students as they develop their presentation skills, I recommend an effort to examine and understand the seminar situation and cognitively re-interpret any bodily "nerve" symptoms that you experience. Think carefully about the presentation context and what is required of you. What are you fearful of? It is often a good idea to ask yourself what the worst possible outcome could be. More often than not, you will identify something along the lines of going blank or not being able to get your words out, or having a panic attack in front of everyone. I have seen many very anxious students have these kinds of experiences, and in reality, the classes I've been in have all had super supportive students and I myself try to reassure the student in question that everything is fine and that they are among a friendly, caring, and supportive group. When you really think about it, going blank, or not being able to get your words out, or even having a panic attack are usually temporary states and really not that bad in the grand scheme of life! Often, when you've accepted what the worst-case scenario is and have realized that it's not that bad, your general anxiety about the whole thing will be reduced. The more you think about the seminar context and what you want to get out of it, the more you can focus on achieving the outcomes that you desire from being in the course, and the less room you have for worry. In short, a sharp focus on goals and a plan to achieve them leaves less mental capacity for worrying. Sometimes though, just thinking through worst-case scenarios is not enough, and you will actually need some tools to utilize when you feel anxious or stressed. An excellent resource for learning all about how to overcome anxiety, worry, panic, and other common negative thought patterns is a book called *Thoughts and feelings: Taking control of your moods and your life*, by Matthew McKay, Martha Davis, and Patrick Fanning. I strongly recommend this book, even for students who think they've got it all figured out. It contains enormously useful information that you can use to get more in touch with reality and reduce the burden of troublesome thoughts. Over the years, I have polled students about what they fear in a seminar context and basically the list boils down to the following four main points:

1. Fear of looking "stupid" or "unintelligent"
2. Fear of going blank, not knowing what to say, and having a panic attack
3. Fear of being asked hard questions
4. Non-specific: I don't know why I am so nervous; I just am

The good news is that these things are 100 per cent beatable! The not-so-good news is you won't overcome these fears without putting in time and effort, and working smartly, not randomly. But that's true of everything; nothing that's worthwhile is easy.

The fact of the matter is that, fundamentally, fear of failure is heavily related to insufficient preparation. The issue, though, is that many students don't understand the degree of preparation required to beat their fear of failure and really do an amazing job of presenting. They also often don't appreciate that structured preparation helps to deal with all the fears they may have. Of course, there will always remain a small risk that something in the presentation can go wrong. However, a key component of preparation is contingency planning—and this is where structured visualization comes in very handy indeed. You might not be able to do a practice presentation and experience everything that could go wrong, but you can imagine it, and imagine how you will deal with it—successfully!

To repeat, quite simply, all of the four fears listed above can be overcome with solid preparation. If you learn the material you are going to present inside-out, your self-confidence with it will be enhanced to the extent that you are not scared of forgetting anything or going blank. The key is to *over-learn the material*, and not just by rote memory, but really understand the material. You can only do this by considering the material carefully, explaining it to non-experts, and re-explaining it until you understand the very core components of the ideas. Forget about terminology and memorization in this process. The key is to understand the concepts that are fundamental to your presentation. You should practice explaining the core concepts to yourself, your friends, your family, or whoever will listen to you. Run your understanding by the professor as well if you like. If they tell you you've got it, that in itself is a massive confidence booster.

The Ultimate Preparation: Planning for the "No-slides" Scenario and Using Structured Visualization

So, you have a fear of going blank or looking dumb. How would these fears manifest and what can you do to overcome them? Going blank is a common fear; I've even had a student say to me when I've asked a question in question period that her mind just "went blank." This of course is possible and can happen to even the very best prepared student (or professor) in the world. However, the probability that this will happen can be reduced to near zero through preparation. One way to avoid this from happening is to maintain your focus on what you are saying and to think ahead of time about the different types of questions you could get on the topic you are presenting. An approach I have found useful is to go through every single slide in the presentation and ask yourself what questions could arise about material on that particular slide. When you've thought about this ahead of time, there is much less chance of going blank if someone does ask something. Chances are, you've already thought about it!

In order to bolster your confidence and get information into your head so you "know it," over-learning the thread of your talk is key. A potential scenario that I always tell students to think about is the situation where the projector and computer for some reason don't work. What would you do? Can you still give your talk? You have no slides and no presenter's notes. One way to prepare for this possibility is to practice your presentation to the point where you can do it without notes and even without slides if you have to. It never hurts to stash some cue cards in your backpack to use in the unlikely event of technical catastrophe. However, the real goal is to be able to give your talk without any resources other than a whiteboard.

To be clear, in addition to practicing your presentation with the slides as normal, practicing without slides or notes is an additional form of preparation that you should do. Pretend that you only have a chalkboard or a whiteboard, and nothing else. Can you draw the essential ideas out? Can you illustrate the main results? If you prepare to be able to do this if necessary, you massively reduce the risk of "going blank" and a huge bonus is that your self-confidence with the material will skyrocket. This is because you have not simply "remembered" what you have to say, you have understood it in all its complexity, and you can explain the concepts without the need for fancy terms or language to explain it. You get it and could explain it to a child.

Remember, when self-confidence is high, you will approach the achievement situation with a much better attitude. In fact, if you have prepared to the point where you can deliver the main points clearly without slides, you pretty much have nothing to fear in the presentation environment itself. An everyday saying from the boxing world is appropriate here: "Train hard, fight easy." Loosely translated, this means the harder you push yourself and test your limits in preparation, the easier it will be on the day, when the limits and challenges are less than what you put yourself through in preparation.

Just as you can contingency-plan for the "no-slides" scenario, you can contingency-plan for almost every eventuality. A great method for doing this involves imagining how you would successfully deal with various issues. Begin by listing all possible questions and things that you fear could go wrong during the presentation, and imagine yourself answering them and dealing with them well. You can do this for every kind of situation. Imagine a particularly arrogant peer is in the class and tends to ask very condescending questions. How would you deal with this? Imagine yourself calmly responding with the appropriate information and not being reactive and responding impolitely. The good thing about visualization is that you can use it in myriad different ways. You don't have to always use it to plan for the worst! You can simply imagine yourself going through the presentation slide-by-slide, point-by-point, and doing a great job. The great thing is that you can even do this kind of preparation when lying in bed. The benefits are huge—don't underestimate the power of visualization. Be careful though: always imagine yourself doing things well, responding to questions with confidence and knowledge. Research has shown that imagining yourself doing badly can lead to bad performance (Woolfolk et al., 1995). Thus, do not envisage failures or screw-ups. However, do envisage how you will transcend "potential" screw-ups with ease and poise. I cannot recommend visualization for seminar preparation enough!

Use Self-Talk and Cognitive Restructuring

You are a few minutes from having to present. Your heart races, your mouth is dry, you have butterflies in your stomach, and you are sweating. Are you scared or are you intensely excited? Technically, you could be either and to some extent you have a choice in the way you cognitively interpret these bodily symptoms. Many students find themselves panicking when they experience these normal bodily responses to a challenging situation or an achievement situation. They then talk themselves into a worse state of anxiety and stress. Perhaps their inner voice says, "That's it, I know I'm going to screw up." The great news is that it is relatively easy to change the way you interpret these bodily symptoms by changing what you say to yourself. Try telling yourself that these signs are necessary in order to make you perform your best. If you weren't a bit nervous, you wouldn't perform to the best of your ability. In fact, there is a well-known relationship between arousal and performance called the "inverted-U hypothesis" (Arent

& Landers, 2003). This idea holds that when arousal levels are low, performance will be sub-par. The same is true when arousal levels are very high. Luckily, though, there is a sweet spot of arousal (the peak of an inverted U) at which performance will be optimal. By this view, experiencing no arousal before a performance situation is worse than feeling some arousal. Telling yourself that arousal is good for you may be hard to do at first. However, the technique of self-talk in conjunction with solid preparation as outlined above is nothing short of miraculous. Many high-level performers cannot perform well unless they are physically sick prior to an event! Nerves are okay to have. The key is to remain focused on what you know you have to do and what you have prepared for, and not be baited into thinking of the million different ways things could go horribly wrong. Cognitive restructuring is a closely related concept and involves using self-talk to change your thoughts. So, if, when you felt your heart race you thought, "That's it, I know I'm going to screw up," you could potentially change this thought to a coping statement like, "My heart is racing; I can do this," or an even more positive statement like, "My heart is racing; I know I'm going to ace this." If you have prepared using practice and structured visualization which includes contingency planning for things that "could" go wrong, you really have nothing to fear. So when you detect those butterflies, tell yourself that they're a sign that you are going to do a great job!

If You're Overly Anxious Prior to Presenting, Use Relaxation Techniques to Calm Yourself Down

Anxiety is a normal response, and can be effectively dealt with via the use of relaxation techniques. The simplest and perhaps quickest form of relaxation is breath control. It can be done in a matter of a minute or two and is effective in re-setting your body just prior to presentation. Breath control consists of an inhalation phase in which you breathe in slowly through your nose, noticing how your diaphragm presses down. During this phase you should focus on breathing from your stomach, which you should notice pushing outward fully. This inhalation stage should last about five seconds. During the exhalation phase, breathe slowly out through your mouth. The muscles in your neck and shoulders should relax. You should breathe out very slowly for about seven seconds (Weinberg & Gould, 1995). Repeating this simple breathing exercise a few times can help bring you back to a better state of readiness prior to your presentation.

Another method for relatively quick on-the-spot relaxation is derived from a technique called Progressive Muscular Relaxation (PMR). This technique involves tensing then relaxing the major muscle groups in your body in a set order. Whereas the usual PMR approach can take a long time, there is a shorter version for quick relief from stress. In the shortened version, you divide your body up into four areas; arms, head, legs, and trunk and start by clenching your fists and tensing your arms. You hold this for seven seconds, then relax for 20 seconds. Next, you contract all your facial muscles so as to scrunch up your face as much as possible, hold for seven seconds, and then relax. After your head, you move onto your trunk. Arch your back and take a deep breath (be careful not to over-arch) and hold this pose for a few seconds, then relax. After taking another deep breath, push your stomach out as you breathe in, then relax. Finally, move onto your legs and extend your toes upwards, tighten your lower leg muscles, then relax. Follow this by clenching your glute muscles and your quadriceps, then relax. This whole sequence should only take a couple of minutes and is helpful as a means of reducing tension and stress held in your body. It takes practice, though. McKay, Davis & Fanning (2011) suggest that you require approximately 7 to 14 PMR practice sessions to get quite good at identifying muscle tension and releasing it. When you've become proficient at this technique, you'll be able to scan your body to identify tense muscles and relax them without the need to pre-tense them on purpose.

You can also use these relaxation techniques over a more extended time period to relax and de-stress when you are not just about to present. For example, using these techniques the night before an anxiety-provoking event can be very helpful in helping you get to sleep. If you tend to worry and feel stressed all the time, I strongly recommend that you incorporate regular exercise, yoga, and mindfulness meditation into your normal routine. It is good to note that in the modern age, these activities are becoming accepted essential components of physical and mental health.

Meditation is a useful strategy that can help calm you down and reduce anxiety. One particular type of meditation involves watching your thoughts. There are numerous techniques to do this kind of meditation and I will just highlight one here. Sit down in a comfortable position, close your eyes, and focus on your breath. Notice how your lungs expand and contract, and your ribs and diaphragm also expand and contract as you breathe. Really focus your attention on the physical experience of breathing. Even though you are trying to focus on your breath, thoughts will continue to pop into your head. The key with this meditative exercise is not to get attached to any thought that enters your awareness. Instead, acknowledge thoughts as they arise and then let them go and return your focus to your breath. You will experience a constant tussle between keeping your attention on your breath and acknowledging thoughts as they arise. However, by not indulging your thoughts, you can get a sense that they are not the only things that define you. You can be an impartial observer of your thoughts and thereby reduce the grip that they otherwise can have on you. Practice this form of thought watching for five minutes initially, and increase the time as you get better. This simple exercise can help to gain a deeper insight into how thoughts can take over at any given moment and how you can reduce the likelihood of "buying into them," just by acknowledging them and re-focusing on something else. If you are a chronically anxious person, this form of mind training is extremely valuable.

Even for well-adjusted students, university can be a stressful experience and there is every reason to use this experience to develop holistic life skills. The ideas I've presented in this section can be found on almost any website or in any book on dealing with stress and anxiety, but I strongly recommend the book by McKay and colleagues that I mentioned earlier. The book also includes a great chapter on worry control—just what you might need if you tend to get really worried about presentations or speaking in class. There is a huge amount of fantastic advice given in this book about how to overcome stress and anxiety, be mindful, relax, and get things into perspective. I strongly urge you to go out and pick up a copy at your local bookstore. The tips and advice will help you attain holistic well-being and will help you even "well" beyond your university tutorial and seminar experience.

Concentrate on What You Must Do, Not What You Must Not Do

As I mentioned previously, imagining yourself doing badly will lead to a drop in performance (Woolfolk et al., 1985). So, at all costs, avoid imagining yourself doing badly! Think and focus only on what you must do, not what you must not do. By being mindful, that is, monitoring your mental state, you can "catch" yourself before you slide down the slippery slope to imagining failure. Failure should not be in your mind. Remember, you have planned for everything, you can give this presentation without slides if you need to, and you can explain the concepts to a total novice. Tell yourself that you will do great and chances are, you will!

A Note to Shy Students

Shyness has been defined as a tendency to avoid social situations and to fail to participate appropriately in social situations (Pilkonis, 1977). Many students are shy and feel very apprehensive both when required to present or participate in class discussions in seminar or in tutorial situations. The good news is that, while being shy might be your natural tendency, there are steps you can take to become more effective in these types of achievement situations. There is nothing wrong with being shy, and you should not feel as though there is something "wrong" with you. Research has shown that on average across multiple cultures, around 40 per cent of people classify themselves as being shy—so, you are definitely not alone (Carducci & Zimbardo, 1995).

A particularly relevant component of shyness is the idea that shy individuals are sometimes overly self-conscious and have a feeling that they are being heavily scrutinized by others (Buss, 1980). Compared to their more outgoing counterparts, shy people tend to be more concerned about what others will think of them. Therefore, a useful tip for overcoming shyness is to focus on something other than how you think others are seeing you. Some people recommend turning self-consciousness into self-awareness. Get to know yourself, and analyze which situations make you shyer than others. Try not to think about how others are seeing you. You will be glad to know that most people are far too busy thinking about themselves to spend excessive effort thinking about others. When someone else is talking, try focusing on them with as much concentration as you can muster; listen to them intently and focus on their expressions and personality. What do you like about them? What are they trying to say? Is there anything you can learn from the way they present themselves? Similarly you can scrutinize how others in your group interact socially.

I know all this is easier said than done for many shy individuals. I've spoken with shy individuals and heard first-hand how they just can't seem to get the words out when they have to talk in front of others. One exercise that has been used in previous work on public speaking training is to prepare yourself in stages (Fremouw & Zitter, 1978). Start off by reading a passage from a book loudly and clearly, with a focus on intonation. You can start by doing this seated, then progress to doing it standing up, then try paraphrasing the passage without reading it, and finally try to articulate spontaneous speech. When you can do this well alone, try doing it in front of one other person. Exercises like this can help you to gradually reduce the aversion you have to speaking in front of others.

When you are in a group discussion situation, try asking simple questions first to get yourself into the conversation. A question doesn't have to be complicated; a simple "What do you think about X?" question can really help in getting you into the conversation, and putting the onus on the other person to provide their opinion. You can set yourself "contribution" goals for each tutorial or seminar. Say, for example, that you would like to contribute one "big" point to the discussion and a minor point as well. In preparation for the discussion, practice asking the questions or raising the points. Be sure to speak clearly and deliberately and imagine making eye contact with the professor or with another student in class that you get along with. By imagining talking with a friend in class in this way, you can turn a potentially scary group discussion situation into a discussion with a friend. Much less daunting! You can use visualization to imagine the nerves you think you would feel in class and overcome them through deep breathing, self-talk, or another strategy. Remember, visualization is so powerful—it's like being able to do a dry run prior to the real thing. Using visualization, you can prime yourself to act a certain way by imagining yourself acting that way. So, visualize yourself being very competent in social situations and responding positively when asked a question. Imagine yourself explaining a concept eloquently in a clear voice. Try hard to make eye contact with the person you are communicating with. This is often enough to help you engage and talk to them. Focusing on one person helps you to avoid thinking about what the other people in the group might be thinking.

When you are talking, focus on the message you are trying to deliver, not on what you think others are thinking about you. Keeping focused on what you're saying and sticking to your prepared plan helps avoid the pitfalls of beginning to think too much about how others see you. The key is really to avoid over-scrutinizing yourself and realize that everyone else is also scrutinizing themselves, and so in all likelihood not scrutinizing you. If you are really worried at the end of a class that you haven't managed to contribute to the discussion in the way you wanted to, approach the professor after class with something along the lines of: "I really wanted to make a point in the discussion but I couldn't get myself into the conversation, but what I was thinking about that paper was *XYZ*. Do you think this makes sense? I was thinking about it in the light of the research we were talking about by Blogs et al....." Although you've approached the professor after class, you've clearly signalled that you've thought about the topic and you wanted to get a point across but for some reason couldn't. This registers with professors and might help improve your grade on the odd class where you couldn't say much. However, you can't rely on this strategy in every class!

Last but not least, don't worry about conforming. The fact that you are shy is no different than the fact that someone else is not shy. Yes, in certain situations you see your shyness as a limitation, but believe me, many outgoing individuals get themselves into way more trouble by talking too much at the wrong times. There are many useful books and resources on the internet providing useful tips and strategies for overcoming shyness and building confidence. Many universities also offer workshops and help with learning how to present more effectively and overcome shyness and fear of public speaking. Look them up and don't be afraid to try out different things. But always remember, this is something you are doing to help you function better in certain situations; there is nothing intrinsically wrong with being shy. It is part of what makes you unique as an individual.

Leading and Contributing to Group Discussions

Class discussions are an important part of the tutorial and seminar experience. Often, the person presenting a paper or proposal will also be required to lead a class discussion on the topic. Correspondingly, the instructor will be looking for the quality of input from the rest of the class during the discussion. The quality and quantity of input often go into a calculation of "participation" marks which are subsequently factored into the final grade. Is there a method for success in either leading or contributing to class discussion? In my view, "method" may be too strong a word, but there are certainly several important things to consider when it comes to doing well in class discussions.

When leading a class discussion, it is important for the leader to play a guiding and facilitative role. Therefore, having five or more talking points prepared ahead of time is key—assuming five minutes per point, this gives you 25 minutes of discussion material. A good approach to leading is to begin with a brief summary of the main points in the presentation, and then present a specific question for discussion. You should make sure that the questions you pose are not simple yes/no questions, as that would kill the discussion pretty quickly. Another thing to bear in mind is that silence is acceptable. I always tell my seminar students that there is no such thing as an awkward silence in small group classes. Thinking time is absolutely fine, and as a leader, you shouldn't panic if there are several seconds or even a minute or so between you posing the discussion point or question and receiving a response. If you feel that it really is taking too long for a contribution to appear, you can bridge the thinking time with reassuring comments like, "It's ok, take your time; when I first thought about this question it took me ages to figure it out." When someone actually contributes a thought, be careful not to get into a "private" chat with them and thereby ignore the rest of the group. Try to open up the discussion to the rest of the group with sentences like, "That's a really interesting approach; what do you guys think of that idea?" If you want to be really innovative, you could come up with a scheme to really get people into the discussion, perhaps by framing the topic as a debate and assigning people to one side or the other. It is also useful to paraphrase peoples' contributions to make sure that you understood their point and to give everyone else a second chance to understand the point being made. Given the diversity of personalities in a typical seminar or tutorial setting (ranging from shy to very outgoing), it will usually be impossible to create the perfect discussion environment for everyone. The best you can do is be sensitive to the different people in the room. Also, by being more directed in some of your questions (that is, addressing them toward specific people), you can maximize your chances of engaging as many people as possible in the discussion.

In seminars and tutorials the onus is on each and every student to come to class prepared to contribute to a discussion on the topic under study. As mentioned above, for many shy students, contributing to discussions can be a difficult thing to do, but given the general real-world importance of being able to work effectively and communicate in a group, my strong recommendation is for shy students to set themselves contribution goals. One way of doing this is to set increasingly more difficult goals as the semester progresses. You could begin by having a modest goal of making a couple of small contributions initially and gradually building up over a period of weeks until you are able to make several contributions per discussion. Many of the points I made above for shy students are highly relevant to anyone (shy or not) trying to "get in" on the conversation. Notwithstanding shyness levels, here's a list of 10 pointers to bear in mind when considering how to contribute to class discussion(s):

1. Prepare well. Critical appraisal of the paper or topic under study is important to good preparation. This happens before you even turn up to class. You should have notes in hand and potential questions and comments pre-written.

2. Make notes. It is crucial to have a notepad or laptop with you and make notes while the presenter is speaking. This helps draw connections between what they are saying and what you read in the paper. You should also note down thoughts as other people are talking.

3. Once you have a point you want to get across, rehearse silently in your head how you'll say it. This is multitasking in action— you are half listening to the ongoing conversation and half focusing on how you'll put your point across.

4. When exchanging different viewpoints with classmates, keep emotions in check and stay focused on the topic, not personal digs! This sounds far-fetched but I have seen students (and faculty) get quite stressed out while they are defending a point they've made or critiquing someone else's point. This some-times leads to questionable tones and demeanour.

5. Don't interrupt. You may have worked out the perfect response to someone else's input, but exercise patience and politeness at all times. Letting people speak is basic common courtesy.

6. Be honest about what you think, but be diplomatic and respectful. Some may say that "hard" talking is part of the cut and thrust of academia, but my own view is that diplomatic communication is far better than unedited straight talk. Don't get me wrong—it is perfectly possible to be firm, critical, and challenging, while at the same time being diplomatic.

7. Don't take over the conversation. I have seen this many times in student discussions—one or two talkers dominate the con-versation and other members of the group have a hard time getting a word in. Be cognizant of the relative contributions of different group members and provide some gaps in your talking to let others into the conversation.

8. Don't be afraid to ask other class members for clarification or an example to illustrate a point they have made. If you find it difficult to think fast during a conversation, this is an easy way to get into the chat. Ask a simple question such as: "I'm not sure I followed what you said; could you give an example to clarify what you meant?"

9. Use body language effectively. Use non-verbal cues to show others you are listening to them. Nodding, making eye contact,

and leaning in are excellent ways to show others that you are engaged with what they are saying. Likewise, when you are speaking use eye contact and make visual contact with various members of the group.

10. Be humble but not self-deprecating. There is a fine line between humility and self-deprecation. False humility can also be annoying to other people. Whenever scientists discuss the physical or social world, it is appropriate to do so with a certain amount of sincere humility because there are countless things that we just don't understand yet. However, being falsely humble or making statements such as, "I'm always wrong in this class, but I think that *XYZ* . . ." doesn't come across well. Rather say something like, "I'm not sure if this is on the mark, but what about *XYZ*," or, "I'm not an expert on this topic but from the limited reading that I've done, does *XYZ* make sense?"

This section has highlighted a potentially fruitful way to go about delivering a research paper presentation. Remember, you might be asked to do other kinds of presentations, but the guidelines given here should help with those too. Finally, also bear in mind that the guidelines given here are just that: guidelines. They are not hard and fast rules and there are many other ways in which to prepare and deliver effective presentations. If you have a great idea that doesn't align with my suggestions in this and the previous chapter, talk to your professor about it. If they are supportive, go for it!

Recommended Further Reading

Esposito, J.E. (2007). *In the spotlight: Overcoming your fear of public speaking and performing*. Bridgewater, CT: In the Spotlight LLC.

Feldman, D.B., & Silvia, P.J. (2012). *Public speaking for psychologists: A light-hearted guide to research presentations, jobs talks, and other opportunities to embarrass yourself*. Washington, DC: American Psychological Association.

Miller, F. (2011). *No sweat public speaking: How to develop, practice and deliver a knock your socks off presentation with no sweat*. St. Louis, MO: Fred Co.

McKay, M., Davis, M., & Fanning, P. (2011). *Thoughts and feelings: Taking control of your moods and your life* (4th ed.). Oakland, CA: New Harbinger Publications.

4
Writing a Paper

Writing as a Vehicle for Idea Transmission

Communication is a critical component of success in virtually any field or work domain. Whether in its written or spoken form, good communication is fundamental to the effective transmission of ideas. If you think about it, university life revolves around the transmission of ideas. However, it takes more than simply verbalizing an idea to convince a thoughtful and reflective person of your perspective. What people need in order to accept an idea is a good argument as to why the idea is worthy of deep consideration. Idea transmission can take place through formal lectures where a professor talks and students listen, or increasingly through a more interactive discussion that often occurs in the setting of seminars and tutorials. Within individual research groups, lab meetings are a chance for members of the research group to talk openly about ideas. Anyone who's been in such meetings will realize that some people seem to be more effective at transmitting their ideas than others. The same is true of professors giving lectures—even a brief look at any of the online professor rating sites will show that some professors seem to have the communication thing down to a fine art, whereas others seem to require more work in this area. Again, when professors lecture or write books and when students do presentations or write papers they are transmitting their ideas to each other and providing compelling arguments to support those ideas. Without good quality communication, idea transmission would be completely compromised and the function of university (or in fact any other organization in which idea transmission is crucial) would be undermined.

Despite the critical importance of communication as a means for idea transmission, it can be an uphill battle getting students (and indeed professors) to realize that their skills could be improved. In recent discussions with a respected colleague who teaches an undergraduate writing course, I've been surprised to learn about how difficult it can be to get students to appreciate the importance of good writing, or to get them to accept that their writing needs improvement. Some, it seems, are tempted to conclude that communication skills are secondary to "primary" technical skills required in different fields. Although there might be a grain of truth in this perspective, for two individuals who possess similar levels of knowledge, it will be the one who can successfully communicate their knowledge to others who will inevitably get ahead. Indeed, it may even be possible for a person with less knowledge to outperform someone else with greater knowledge but a poorer ability to transmit that knowledge.

Written communication in particular is fundamental to many academic and work activities. Professors routinely have to write grant proposals and research papers, executives have to prepare written briefs or reports, and students, of course, have to write papers and exams in their courses. In this chapter, we'll spend some time thinking about what makes idea transmission more effective, with a focus on writing. We consider ideas on how to structure a paper, how to make arguments, and how to construct a paragraph right down to how to formulate a good sentence. I'll try to emphasize the importance of planning and thinking skills and the beauty and effectiveness of keeping things simple. Or to be more specific and to use a famous quote from Albert Einstein, we'll focus on "making things as simple as possible, but not simpler." So let's dive in!

Written Papers in Seminars and Tutorials

Students in seminar and tutorial classes should expect to have to write something during the course. Obviously, depending on how creative your professor is, you could be asked to write different types of paper. Over the years, I've heard of professors asking students to write many different styles of paper including the following:

1. A paper on a certain topic (assigned or chosen): the professor or the student chooses a topic and writes a paper of a specified length on that topic.
2. A research proposal: the student surveys the literature in a given area and writes a proposal outlining a potential research project that addresses a gap in knowledge.
3. A critique of an existing research paper from the literature: the student reads a paper from a particular literature and provides a critical analysis.
4. A position statement for or against an idea or theory: the student is given an idea or theory and is requested to write a paper either in favour or against the idea or theory, and, where appropriate, suggest viable alternatives to the idea or theory.
5. A précis of a pre-existing paper or book: a short summary of a paper or book.
6. A book review: a longer critical analysis of an entire book, typical of what might appear in a journal or magazine.
7. A mini-grant proposal: a mock application for a fictitious grant in which the student is encouraged to stress the importance of their proposed project and why it is deserving of funding.
8. A white paper advocating a change in policy: a critical overview of a field of study that is relevant to social policy along with a list of recommendations for how future policies should change.
9. A literature review: a detailed summary of a field of study, usually involving short summaries of individual papers in a particular area of study.
10. A letter to the editor about a certain paper or topic: the student writes a letter outlining their perspective on a target article or topic, assigned by the professor.

While these assignments are all unique, the core skills required to write something good are common to all. It is these core skills, and not the nuances of the myriad different formats you might be asked to write, that we will focus on here. Without exception, each type of assignment in the list above requires effective idea transmission supported by solid arguments. This is true whether the idea pertains to a self-generated research question or material generated by someone else. In all cases, the fundamental question is, "How do I write a compelling piece on the topic?"

Bottom Line
Good writing in the social sciences boils down to effective idea transmission supported by solid arguments that are well presented.

The Personal Nature of Writing

Writing is an incredibly personal activity. Many people get immense joy when putting their thoughts down in their own unique way. The rise of blogging is testimony to this, and it seems that people enjoy reading the thoughts and ideas of bloggers just as much as bloggers enjoy blogging. Many different forms and styles of writing can be effective, so one thing I want to stress is to be wary of overly prescriptive or formulaic advice on how to write. Don't get me wrong, there are some fundamentals to think about, but there should always be ample room to personalize the approach and make your work unique.

The first question that a budding writer might ask themselves is, "Should I make a plan/outline, or just start writing?" This is a very good question and one that deserves some consideration. There are some individuals who believe that the act of writing is the last part of the harder process of idea formulation. These individuals believe that ideas and thoughts should be formulated and structured in lengthy planning sessions, perhaps in bullet form, and that these ideas should then be filled out during the "actual" writing process. By this view, the hard thinking is done before putting the proverbial pen to paper. Others believe that thinking and writing are so intertwined that they must happen in parallel. These individuals believe that to think, they need to start writing. It used to be the case that people would say, "I need a pen in my hand to think," whereas now people say, "I need to be at my computer with the word processor open to think." I want to underline that these two seemingly dichotomous ways of viewing the writing process are not in fact mutually exclusive. Indeed, my own personal style usually involves formulating a loose plan—a skeleton plan if you like—before starting to write prose. However, and critically, I also give myself the freedom to deviate from this plan if the writing process leads my thoughts in a different direction. For example, for many of the chapters in this book, I first created a mind map of what I considered to be essential elements to be included, along with notes on where I would get the background information for specific ideas (for example, other books or papers that I referred to when writing this guide). Only then did I start writing in Microsoft Word. Very often, I found myself deviating from my plan. In some cases I included things that weren't on the original mind map and in others I omitted things that were on the original mind map. The lesson, if there is one, is to be flexible throughout the writing process. Plans are useful but can (and often should) be revised. I think it is a mistake to consider hard thinking as limited to the planning phase. You need to be thinking all the time, because sometimes it is only once you've started trying to fully articulate your ideas that you realize they are ill conceived or just plain wrong.

Before you can plan the content and flow of your paper, you need to know a little bit about how papers are generally structured. However, before you even think about the details of structure, it is vital that you carefully consider the *people* and the *purpose* for which you are writing. Writing a paper for a professor is quite different from writing a mock article for a newspaper aimed at the general public. Obviously, you can use specialized technical terms (if necessary) for your professor, because she or he will know what they mean, whereas you can't assume any specific background knowledge for a public (non-specialist) audience. We'll get more into style and use of specialized terms and phrases later in the chapter, but for now, just think about the importance of writing for a person and a purpose. These two pieces of information should guide you through the whole process of putting your paper together no matter what kind of paper you are developing. For example, it is only if you have a well-defined purpose that you can tell halfway through your writing that the paper is veering off course and will not fulfil its purpose. I recommend that you use what I call the three P's when starting any piece of written work: People → Purpose → Plan. That is to say, first consider the audience and the purpose and *then* start planning with those two things in mind!

Researching, Planning, and Structuring a Paper

Researching your topic is a key part of the process of planning your paper. Bear in mind that you cannot plan something if you don't know what kind of literature is out there on the topic you are intending to write about. Thus, I recommend that prior to even starting to draft a plan for your paper you perform a literature review using the databases identified earlier in this guide. By spending time reviewing the literature you will be better equipped to pinpoint your topic and identify the scope of your paper. For example, if there is a voluminous literature on a topic spanning a hundred years of research, you will have to be very selective on what your focus is. Here are some questions you may want to ask yourself as you do the first inspection of the literature:

1. How much work has there been on the topic? How many papers were published in the last two to three decades?
2. What are the sub-themes within the main topic? Have papers tended to focus on one particular question, or are there multiple questions that have been addressed in different experiments?
3. How many useful review papers are there? Is there a recent one that synthesizes previous work in an accessible manner? These review papers can be an invaluable source of information for you as you try to sort through the details of the topic.

4. What should the scope of your paper be? Limited to one type of question? Limited to a few questions from the research literature?
5. Are you required to provide a critical analysis or simply give an overview of the area?
6. If you are required to provide a critical analysis, are there specific papers that have done this before that you can refer to?

You can use these six questions as headings as you make notes during your literature review. By the end of this review, you should have identified what the approximate scope of your paper should be. "Scope" refers to the amount of material you want to cover. Do you want to give a high level overview or survey of the whole field? Doing so will necessitate only a very superficial coverage of most issues. In many cases, you will want to hone your focus onto particular topics and sub-themes within a field of study. The critical decision when planning is to figure out which sub-themes you want to focus on. A narrow scope is fine, as long as you provide justification in your paper for why you chose to limit your consideration to a particular sub-topic or theme. This is a very important point so I will repeat it and emphasize it some more: You should *always* be thinking about justifying your approach, especially if you choose an unorthodox or unusual topic or scope. If the professor or grader is kept guessing as to why you took the approach that you did, they might be inclined not to reward you for your creativity, or to think you didn't have a broad appreciation of the area. On the other hand, if you specify why you took a particular approach, there is no room left for misinterpretation of your motives. This doesn't mean you have to write specific messages to your grader in the paper, only that you should explain why you are focusing on one part but not another of a particular topic. For example, if you are a psychology or neuroscience student, your topic could be "the mirror neuron system." There are many different questions and sub-themes within this broad topic. You might decide to focus only on the issue of whether research on the mirror system tells us anything about social deficits in individuals with autism spectrum conditions. Rather than just diving into this topic, you might consider a justification as follows:

Since their discovery, mirror neurons have been studied by many researchers and the questions asked by these researchers have been diverse. For example, some authors have theorized about the origins of mirror neurons, whereas others have investigated whether mirror neurons can be driven by auditory as opposed to visual input, and yet others have focused on whether mirror neurons respond to actions involving tools. However, in this paper, I focus on the specific question of whether abnormalities in mirror system function might explain some of the social deficits observed in individuals with autism spectrum conditions.

The strength of the above paragraph is that the reader has not been left wondering whether you are aware of the breadth of sub-topics within the study of the mirror system. This type of justification demonstrates both that you are aware of the breadth of topics within the main topic and that you are purposely narrowing the focus to a particular issue.

Imagine instead you had dived straight in with:

Many believe that autism spectrum conditions might be in part due to deficits in mirror system function. For example, a study by *XYZ* showed that *ABC* . . .

Whereas you may have gone on to make many good points about the idea of a link between the mirror system and autism spectrum conditions, you have not demonstrated a wider appreciation of the field and have not shown that you have been selective in which aspects you attended to in your paper. In my opinion, a student who takes the first approach has done a better job than the student who takes the second approach. We'll come back to more specific suggestions about how to write later in this chapter, but before that, it is important to think in some detail about the overall structure of a paper.

An Overview of the Funnel Method

Justification of your scope and topic are important, but so is the actual structure of your entire paper. In high school you may have been taught that any good paper needs a beginning, a middle, and an end. This rudimentary idea about structure does little more than state the obvious and is of limited use, although clearly, a paper with a well-defined beginning, middle, and end is better than a paper with absolutely no regard for flow—so it's a start. However, this level of structuring is inadequate for university-level writing. For example you also need to consider what exactly constitutes a good beginning, how arguments and ideas are presented in the middle, and how to tie it all together at the end. A commonly used approach is referred to as the funnel method and essentially consists of starting with a reasonably broad contextualization for the main topic of your paper and whittling down to a specific question or thesis quite quickly, followed by arguments pertaining to your ideas and finally a summary and conclusion (Baker & Gamache, 1998). A classic way to conclude is known as the "inverse funnel" and involves first paraphrasing your question or thesis, and then summarizing your most important arguments and their implications within the context of the wider topic (Northey, Tepperman, and Albanese, 2012). The reason this method of concluding is called the inverse funnel is that it goes from a relatively specific restatement of your thesis to a broader discussion of implications for the topic. If you go with this inverse funnel approach, just be sure not to make your implications too broad at the end as this can reduce the impact of your message. Some people advocate a punchy last sentence, but I simply tell students to avoid making the last sentence too abrupt and end on a tone that is relevant and that reads well.

Usually, when assigned a written paper, you will be provided with constraints such as word count, margin size, font size, line spacing, and so on. A long paper would be somewhere in the region of 5000 words but in my experience it's more usual for a paper to be anywhere from 750 to 3000 words. When thinking about your ideas and supporting arguments, you obviously need to be cognizant of this word limit. Usually, papers require a 12-point font (Times New Roman or Arial are fine) and double spacing. Within these constraints, you can bank on approximately 350 words per page.

When you plan your paper you should think about how much space you will allocate to the different parts. Let's assume you've been asked to write a 1500-word paper. Just to keep things simple, that gives you 10 paragraphs of 150 words each. Doing the math, you can see that after allocating one paragraph to your opening and another to your summary and conclusion, you have 8 paragraphs left to transmit the main ideas and support them with good arguments. This little exercise can help you figure out a rudimentary structure for your paper. Again, this structure is open to change as you begin writing. For example, it might be impossible to have 10 equally sized paragraphs and there are no rules saying you need to have a certain number of paragraphs (except that you shouldn't write 1500 words of continuous prose, of course!).

Once you know how much space you have and roughly how it will be divided up, you can mesh this information with the literature searching and research you have done on the central topic of your paper, then decide which ideas you will present in which paragraphs. One strategy that is sometimes advocated is tabulating information as you read through the literature supporting your paper. You can have multiple columns, for example, with the first column indicating the source, the second column indicating the idea or information from that source, and the third column indicating your thoughts on that piece of information. The fourth column could be used for any other notes about that particular piece of information. When it comes to stringing ideas together, some people like being able to refer to such a table. However, I will stress again that this approach may not work for everyone—writers are free to use whatever approach best suits them when writing. They will be judged only on the final outcome of their work.

In terms of ordering of information, some people suggest presenting your weakest ideas and arguments first, and building up to your strongest ones, which should be presented just before the summary and conclusion paragraph. While this is good advice, I believe this tip should be balanced against the need to make each argument as strong as it can be and to employ an order that optimizes the flow and coherence of the paper. This means you might have to play around with the ordering of sentences within paragraphs and paragraphs within the larger paper quite a bit before you get it right. When doing this, you should ask whether each successive idea fits well in the context of what you've written so far. That is, even though each idea or point made in a single paragraph is specific to that paragraph, it should be cohesive with the rest of the paper. Someone reading it should not think, "Where did this come from?" Having outlined one method for creating an overall structure, let's talk some more about the specific sections in the paper.

A Good Start

A good start is crucial to any paper. When employing the funnel method, one thing to avoid is making your beginning too broad as this will not tie well into your focus and the reader is essentially kept in the dark about your actual topic for longer. It should be obvious that keeping your reader in the dark for a long time is probably not a good idea when writing a paper with a set word limit. If your topic is the parliamentary system in politics, for example, you could start with a long history of the ways in which societies have been governed since the dawn of time. However, this would a) take a long time (and many words) and b) keep your reader guessing about the main topic of your paper during that time. Instead, you might want to begin with the idea that society needs governance and that many models are possible. You might then give an example of a non-parliamentary system such as the United States and highlight some of the positives and negatives of this system, before fairly quickly arriving at your topic, which is the parliamentary system.

The funnel in which you start broadly and then narrow down pretty quickly is one approach to starting your paper. When taking this approach a rule of thumb is to get to the specific question or topic by the end of your first paragraph. However, the funnel approach is just one way in which you could structure a paper. Going from a broad to a specific focus in the first paragraph doesn't have to be the approach you take. For example, perusing through newspapers, you'll see many a talented writer start with a controversial or punchy quote. For example, in a piece about the illicit organ trade in developing countries, a newspaper journalist might start with something like:

"There's nothing wrong with taking organs from poor people." These are the words of a backstreet doctor who makes large sums of money selling kidneys removed from the most desperate people in the slums of India.

This kind of opening quote can be a great method for grabbing the reader's attention and piquing their interest. Another way to begin is with a punchy fact such as:

Every minute on earth, more than 250 babies are born.

After grabbing the reader's attention with this "hook," you might then provide a broader context before highlighting the specific focus of your essay.

Note though, when using controversial or punchy beginnings, you need to make sure you stay on topic. Don't make the famous mistake of grabbing the reader's attention with material that is unrelated to your main topic! It's like the classic "Sex, drugs, and rock and roll. . . . Now that I have your attention, let's talk about preservatives used in canned food." It just doesn't work and will annoy your readers—so don't do it.

Finally, another method that is sometimes effective is to start with a quote. For example, I could have started this whole chapter with a quote from Steven Pinker such as, "Speaking and writing involve very different kinds of human relationship, and only the one associated with speech comes naturally to us" (Pinker, 2014, p. 27).

The last sentence or two of your introductory paragraph (or paragraphs if your paper is longer) is commonly referred to as the "thesis statement." The thesis statement basically tells the reader what the main focus of your paper is, and hints at the points you'll consider throughout the piece. When you write the thesis statement, be sure to refer back to how the task was assigned by the professor. What do they want you to achieve with the paper? Address a controversial debate? Critique a specific paper from the literature? Your thesis statement should address the specific purpose of your paper. There are numerous excellent resources available to help students with the development of a thesis statement. One that

I particularly like is on a website run by Purdue University. The website is an amazing resource for writers and contains copious amounts of priceless information. I strongly encourage all students involved in a writing activity to consult this great online resource. The website is called the "Online Writing Lab (OWL)" and can be accessed at: https://owl.english.purdue.edu/.

The sample paper provided in Appendix 2 illustrates how an opening paragraph can be structured.

The Middle of Your Paper—Making Your Arguments

After your beginning, you need to present all the ideas you want to get across. A general rule is to outline one idea per paragraph. It is imperative that each idea you provide is supported by strong arguments. What is an argument? The Oxford dictionary defines an argument as "a reason, or set of reasons given with the aim of persuading others that an action or idea is right or wrong." Notice how this definition has "ideas" and "reasons" at its core. As we've discussed above, a well-written paper is an idea trans-mission vehicle supported by well-made arguments—or reasons. But what exactly is a well-made argument, or a good reason? You know intuitively what a good argument is. We've all had conver-sations in which we've been trying to convince someone of some idea or fact. Famously, not all facts are self-evident; many need to be explained and supported with evidence. We know we've been successful when, despite their best efforts our friend just cannot oppose our idea any longer. When we've made a good argument it is as if the validity of our idea becomes undeniable and the per-son we're talking with simply has to accept it. On the other hand, we know intuitively what a bad argument is too. You probably recognize the situation in which you're floundering trying to con-vince someone of an idea but secretly, even you don't know why you think the idea is a good one, or worse still, you know it is a bad one! There are two types of logical reasoning that you often hear about and it's instructive to consider them briefly. *Induction* refers to a way of presenting arguments in which specific cases or examples are used to support a general conclusion. On the other hand, *deduction* is a way of presenting arguments in which a general theory or truth is applied to a specific case and conclusion about that case. Importantly, in inductive reasoning, the examples or premises are suggestive for a particular conclusion, whereas in deductive reasoning the theory or well-established idea leads directly (not just suggestively) to the conclusion. I am not going to couch the rest of this chapter in terms of inductive and deductive reasoning but knowing about these two common forms of logic is useful for any writer trying to make convincing arguments.

In his excellent recent book on writing, the renowned Harvard psychologist Steven Pinker makes a strong case that a particular cognitive bias, called "the curse of knowledge," is responsible for quite a bit of the bad writing that we encounter every day. The curse of knowledge refers to the difficulty that knowledgeable people have in taking the perspective of less knowledgeable people when trying to explain a particular topic. As Pinker points out, this curse is perhaps best exemplified in the amazingly un-user-friendly product manuals that we receive with some of our most impressive high-tech gadgets. The engineers who designed the gadget in question know how it works better than anyone, but they often cannot appreciate the base level of knowledge that an average user will bring to the table. Writers of user manuals sometimes use overly technical language and lay out sequences of actions in a way that a novice doesn't get. When they do this, they are assuming knowledge that most "average Joes" simply don't possess. Thus, one very important thing to keep in mind when constructing your ideas and arguments for a paper is how best to make everything as clear and understandable as necessary to *your reader*. I have seen students use dozens of technical terms in a paper in an attempt to impress me. Unfortunately, more often than not, the result is the opposite. I am much more impressed with a clear, understandable explanation of the important points and a minimal use of jargon. So be careful! When you've spent considerable time and effort thinking about and researching a particular topic, it is all too easy to assume that your reader will be as familiar as you are, or rather to forget that they have not spent as much time on the topic as you have. It is easy to fall prey to the curse of knowledge. During writing, it is crucial to step outside of yourself to ensure that you don't lose your reader by using overly complex or specialized language. This is easier said than done, though, and the best approach to find out whether what you've written is pitched correctly is to ask a friend or family member who is not as familiar with the topic as you are to read through and provide comments. Just as I do when advising students about how to give oral presentations, I often tell my seminar students to write in such a way that an intelligent high school student can understand the content. This doesn't mean dumbing things down, but rather writing clearly and in easily digestible chunks. The human cognitive system can maintain about three or four chunks of information at once. This means that your writing should be designed not to exceed this processing limitation. For example, if you make several points or place several conditional statements or clauses into one sentence, it will be hard for the reader to keep track. The result: at worst your message or idea is lost, or at best, it's diluted.

Bearing in mind the Oxford definition of an argument, it is vital in any good paper to give reasons as to why you are presenting a particular idea in a paragraph. An idea can be transmitted by making a number of points, each of which are supported by something more than mere guesswork. What kind of support is good support for a point or idea? Well, if there are pertinent studies from the literature, you would do well to cite them. For example, if your point is that pregnancy after the age of 35 is associated with greater risks to both baby and mother than pregnancy prior to the age of 35, your point would be extremely strong if you provide evidence in the form of data showing the statistical links between age and pregnancy-related health issues. One approach I've seen work quite well is to back up ideas with a kind of "one-two punch." What I mean by this is first present the point, then present results from a single study that supports the point, and then to really nail it, highlight a comprehensive review or meta-analysis that shows that the single study you cited is representative of the literature at large. A meta-analysis is a statistical procedure that takes many different results from studies examining the same question and combines them to determine the "big picture" with regard to the question. Meta-analyses can be extremely powerful and reliable sources of information about a particular research question. This is extremely important: with the wealth of sources available in the twenty-first century, it is almost always possible to find a paper or study to support your opinion, no matter what your opinion actually is. In view of this, arguably the most convincing evidence that you could cite is evidence that has been replicated and for which there exists an established consensus. However, finding this kind of evidence is not always possible and sometimes you will have to dig around the literature (using the databases I introduced earlier in the book) and create your own tally of results that support the point you're trying to make.

How about the issue of where ideas and opinions come from? Well, this is an interesting one. In my view, social scientists should, whenever possible, form their opinions based on the evidence available on a particular topic. So, when I mentioned above that it is possible to find evidence to support any opinion, I am not advocating forming an opinion based on mere conjecture and then finding evidence to support it. Instead, I am saying that opinions themselves should emerge from reading and studying the available evidence. In this way, the citing of evidence simply reveals what you are basing your opinion on. However, to form an opinion that will be on firm ground, your review of the relevant literature needs to be extensive. Don't worry though, this doesn't mean that you aren't ever allowed to give any unqualified opinions! In fact, speculation is often the most fun part of writing a scientific paper. I, as well as many other scientists out there, often speculate as to what underlying processes could have caused the pattern of results observed in an experiment. The key is to admit when you are speculating and to avoid organizing a whole paper around speculation.

Some further consideration of what is and what is not a good quality reference is in order at this stage. Let's talk first about the infamous Wikipedia "open" encyclopedia. Let me start by saying that Wikipedia is one of my favourite online resources. However, given that anyone can alter information on the site, it is more susceptible than other more "closed" resources to contamination by bad information. So, my advice to students is to limit the use of Wikipedia to getting a quick overview of a topic or question. Never rely solely on Wikipedia as your source. You must cross-reference and corroborate the information you gather. Just like with the one-two punch approach I recommended above, you cannot simply pull some information from Wikipedia and use it without some other information that supports its reliability and validity. The gold standard type of reference is the peer-reviewed paper, published in an academic journal of good repute. Why is this the gold standard? In two words: peer review. In order for a researcher, such as your professor, to get a scientific paper published, they need to do an experiment or study, write it up, and then submit it to the editor of an academic journal. This editor then sends the paper out to a number of international experts in the field of study (usually two to four) and asks them to read it and critique it (and I mean really critique it; in other words, rip it to shreds). These reviewers then send their comments and criticisms relating to the work back to the editor who makes an initial decision as to whether the paper is worthy of further consideration for publication or should be rejected. The basis for a paper being rejected is usually related to problems with the methodology, or in some cases problems with the very question being asked or the author's interpretation of the data. If the budding author is lucky, the editor will render a "revise and resubmit" decision. Having received such a decision, the author goes back, often collects more data, significantly re-writes the paper, and finally resubmits it to the editor. The editor again sends the revised paper back out to the experts, who again, mercilessly criticize the revision. They then send comments back to the editor and very often the process repeats a couple more times before the editor finally either accepts or rejects the paper. This process can literally take over a year, and with most good journals only a relatively small percentage of submissions are finally accepted. This process is called peer review and is why papers published in peer-reviewed journals are the gold standard type of reference. Books can be a very good source of information too, but it depends on the type of book and whether the material in the book is itself backed up by solid evidence or whether it's mere guesswork or unsubstantiated opinion. Use your judgment as an educated student when picking sources to cite, but always cross-reference and triangulate to strengthen your arguments. This advice is gold! You will get better grades if you pick sources well and demonstrate to your reader that your source material is representative of research in the area.

If you're the type of person who likes to plan out a paper fully prior to writing it, then you can incorporate some of the ideas discussed above into your outline. You can list the individual points you will make that are relevant to each idea in each paragraph, along with a citation or sentence summarizing the reason why that point is sensible. So if your paper is on social mimicry, you could fill out each paragraph with more specific details comprising points to be made and supporting material. The first part of your plan could look something like this:

- Introduction (paragraph 1): Idea to highlight how social humans are, and focus down onto mimicry as a key social skill
  - Point 1: Humans are a social species
    - Supporting argument: cite amount of time we spend in the company of others every day
  - Point 2: Many capabilities contribute to successful social function
    - Supporting argument: cite social cognitive experiments showing capacities necessary to understand others; e.g., theory of mind, perspective taking
  - Point 3: One skill that is vital and ubiquitous is the tendency to mimic the people we're interacting with—this paper will focus on this very important social function
- Idea 1 (paragraph 2): as above, and so on.

This kind of outline would end up being extremely detailed and once complete could be turned into prose to complete the paper. Notice also that two of the points made in this opening paragraph are not supported by citations from the literature. I've talked a lot about references and later in the chapter we'll consider some of the "nuts and bolts" of how to reference previous work in your paper. Having said this though, there are other types of references beyond academic papers that you can use. Referencing is something that students often get hung up on and I've frequently been approached by students worried that they can't write anything at all without support from "the literature." The key is to be sensible: For some points, referring to common experiences can provide compelling support. For example, you don't need a citation from the literature to support the point that "People often laugh at comedy clubs," or that "Wearing shoes that are too small will make your feet hurt." These points support themselves. They don't need support from a scientific study to help people to understand or accept them. So a crucial skill for a good writer is the ability to judge when to provide rigorous scientific justification for a point or idea and when to refer to everyday experience. It's not easy though—sometimes reasoning based on everyday experience is misleading. For example, research shows that we are not always very good at uncovering the reasons why we make certain choices about what to buy. In fact, we sometimes tend to make up reasons for our choices after the choice has been made (this is called "confabulating") and we convince ourselves that these made-up reasons are in fact the actual reasons why we chose as we did. In such cases, studies on choice behaviour from the field of behavioural economics might provide more compelling evidence than our everyday experience. If introspection was always right, we wouldn't need a science of the mind to help understand ourselves; we could just "look" within!

When moving from an outline to actual writing, the prose you create should have two clear properties: good sentence structure and coherent paragraphs that flow well. First, sentences should be well structured and easy to understand, which necessitates good word choice and good grammar. An example of good and bad word choice might be as follows:

BAD:
This precise political heavyweight was accused of malfeasance and was pestered by several overzealous, rancorous media representatives for three years before he left his post.

GOOD:
This politician was accused of corruption and was investigated relentlessly by several journalists for three years prior to his resignation from politics.

Second, sentences within a paragraph should be coherent. That is, you must ensure that the sentences you put together flow into each other in a way that will make sense to the reader. I don't have the space or the inclination to devote a whole chapter to grammar but an example can help illustrate what I mean by sentence structure, flow, and coherence.

Let's consider someone writing about multicultural Canada. They might come up with a few sentences such as the ones below. I have placed a bracketed number before each sentence so I can reference it when I re-write the sentence.

(1) Canada is multicultural and most cities have lots of first-generation immigrants born outside the country. (2) Some of the largest populations come from Eastern Europe and Asia but not Africa, and Canada is a welcoming country because it affords rights to all citizens whatever their race and place of birth. (3) There are only about twenty thousand Nigerian people in Canada but there are more than a million Chinese people. (4) There are lots of Ukrainian Churches in Toronto too. (5) Immigrants often live together within large cities and many believe that this is not good and makes Canada less than what it could be.

To be clear, this is a rather poor paragraph with some pretty bad sentences. Let's consider how we might improve it in terms of sentence construction and coherence of the overall paragraph.

The first sentence (1) contains redundant information: first-generation immigrants are by definition born outside the country they immigrated to. This sentence could be better written as,

Canada is a multicultural country and many Canadian cities have large populations of first-generation immigrants.

The second sentence (2) is unfocused and mixes ideas pertaining to the origins of immigrants with ideas about the welcoming nature of Canada. The sentence is not as coherent as it could be. It could be re-written as two sentences:

Many immigrants to Canada originate from Eastern Europe or Asia, whereas there are far fewer immigrants from Africa.

In general, Canada is a welcoming country and all citizens are afforded the same rights, regardless of their race or country of origin.

The second sentence is also not in the right spot and could be moved to a different place in the paragraph to improve the flow.

The third sentence (3) regarding the numbers of Chinese versus the number of Nigerians is not ideal because it switches the order in which these two groups are mentioned in a previous sentence so that Nigerians are mentioned prior to Chinese. That is, in the previous sentence, Asia was mentioned before Africa, so flow will be better if the same ordering is preserved:

For example, although there are more than one million Chinese Canadians there are less than twenty thousand Nigerian Canadians.

In addition, the sentence is not placed in the right spot within the paragraph. I'll place this sentence differently to improve flow when I reconstruct the paragraph below.

The fourth sentence (4) about Ukrainian churches doesn't really fit although there is a loose connection with the previous point about Eastern Europe. This information could be better integrated, or removed. I will opt to remove it to increase the coherence of the paragraph.

Finally, the fifth sentence (5) is a bit of a disaster. The phrase "immigrants often live together" is ambiguous. Do they live in one big house or several houses on the same street, or several streets in the same neighbourhood? Likewise, the word "many" in the next part of the sentence doesn't allow us to determine whether the writer means many immigrants or many non-immigrants, or many immigrants and non-immigrants. The last phrase is also not very specific and could be tightened up. This sentence could be better written as:

Immigrants from certain countries sometimes settle in particular areas within a city and many non-immigrants believe that this pattern of settlement is detrimental to successful integration into Canadian society.

Together these revised sentences use only four more words than the original set of sentences, and we can now reorder these sentences to increase flow and produce a more coherent paragraph:

> Canada is a multicultural country and many Canadian cities have large populations of first-generation immigrants. In general, Canada is a welcoming country and all citizens are afforded the same rights, regardless of their race or country of origin. Many immigrants to Canada originate from Eastern Europe or Asia, whereas there are far fewer immigrants from Africa. For example, although there are more than one million Chinese Canadians there are less than twenty thousand Nigerian Canadians. Immigrants from certain countries sometimes settle in particular areas within a city and many non-immigrants believe that this pattern of settlement is detrimental to successful integration into Canadian society.

I think most people would agree that this is much improved over the original.

Of course, what I've done here represents just one iteration, going from an original set of sentences to a revised set of sentences. This process can and should be repeated multiple times to arrive at the best possible paragraph. For example, one of the next steps would be to edit and revise the paragraph again to reduce unnecessary words. Good writing doesn't come easy; it requires patience and a desire to tweak toward perfection.

The Importance of Examples

In addition to using references to support points and ideas, you can and should provide examples to *illustrate* them. So, if you are writing about research showing that power is associated with increased risk taking, you might illustrate this point with reference to famous powerful individuals who are known to have engaged in risky behaviour. Or, if you are presenting an idea about confirmation bias, you might use an example of a brand manager who seeks out information confirming her notions of the brand, as opposed to attending to information that is counter to her notions. Examples help with putting your point across in a way that is less abstract and more relatable; it's hard to overuse them. Just as I suggested when I discussed oral presentations, metaphors and analogies can also assist in effective idea transmission, but be careful how you use them. Poorly selected metaphors will make your writing worse, not better.

Bottom Line

The middle of a paper should be filled with paragraphs each making several points around a central idea and for which you articulate good reasons, based on sound evidence. The quality of your points, ideas, reasons, and evidence, in addition to how well sentences flow to create coherent paragraphs, will be key in determining how a reader appraises your paper.

Ending the Paper

I've already alluded to the inverse funnel approach to ending a paper. Again, this involves a re-phrasing of your specific thesis along with some discussion of implications for the wider topic. Many people like to also add a punchy or hard-hitting last sentence, or perhaps even a new question for future research. Some people advocate contrasting the style of this last sentence with the style of the rest of your paper as a nice way to make your ending stand out. So, if you've used relatively complex sentences in much of your paper, you might end with a short and simple take-home. One approach I've seen that works in some situations is to end with two sentences, the first of which offers a speculative opinion on what future research might reveal, and the second of which is short and sweet. An example of this approach could be:

> With the increasing availability of ever more sophisticated 3-D printers, patients with organ diseases may not have to wait at all to have their condition resolved, and the world-wide black market for organs may vanish. Only time will tell.

An ending such as this works both with and without the final sentence, but stylistically, the last sentence is useful in underlining the uncertainty of the preceding speculation. In general, final sentences are a great place to stamp your personal style and personality onto the product you've created. Have fun with it!

A Note on Referencing and Use of Unbiased Language

Two important aspects of writing in the social sciences, whether it is in psychology or anthropology, are referencing and use of unbiased language.

Referencing Using Guidelines from the American Psychological Association (APA)

It is critical for you to be aware of the referencing format that is expected of you from your professor. If not otherwise stated, most social science professors will accept referencing in the style of the American Psychological Association (APA). The APA publishes a style manual, which is available on Amazon and other online bookstores, as well as in university bookstores and libraries. I strongly urge all social science students to buy a copy of this manual and consult it whenever you write a paper. It's hard to commit all the stylistic elements to memory so refreshing your memory by looking at the manual is a worthwhile exercise. I am not going to spend too much time on referencing norms and practices here, other than to point out a few basics.

Referencing papers
Citing a single author in the text:

> It was recently found that *XYZ* (Blogs, 2011) . . .

or:

> Blogs (2011) found that . . .

If an author has written two or more papers in different years, include both years separated by a comma:

It has been found that *XYZ* (Blogs, 2011, 2012) . . .

Citing multiple authors

If there are only two authors, always include both author names:

The research to date shows that *XYZ* (Blogs & Doe, 2011) . . .

or:

Blogs and Doe (2011) found that . . .

Note that the "&" is used between author names when they are written inside parentheses and the "and" is used when the names are written outside parentheses.

If there are three to five authors, APA style dictates that all the authors are cited when the citation is first made, and in subsequent citations the authors are referenced using "et al."

First time:

It was shown that *XYZ* (Blogs, Doe, Duck, Roe, & Silly, 2011) . . .

All subsequent references:

It was shown that *XYZ* (Blogs et al., 2011) . . .

Papers with six or more authors should always be cited using the first author name followed by "et al." Multiple references should be separated by semi-colons:

The trend in the literature has been that *XYZ* (Blogs et al., 2011; Doe & Ruby, 2008) . . .

Referencing websites

When referencing web-based resources simply state the web URL in brackets:

It has been shown that *XYZ* (www.justanexample.com) . . .

Referencing secondary sources

If you are citing a source that has been cited by someone else (technically termed a secondary source), cite in the following way:

> Blogs and Roe showed *XYZ* (as cited in Doe & Silly, 2010) . . .

In this case, you should include the source that you actually read (the secondary source) in your reference list at the end of the paper.

Again, I strongly urge you to spend some time sourcing the APA manual and studying the basic requirements for referencing in scientific writing for the social sciences. The guide now includes information on how to reference web-based information, including sources such as Twitter and Facebook.

Use of Unbiased Language Guidelines

APA style guidelines also recommend reducing or eliminating bias in your writing. Many groups in society suffer from negative stereotypes that are often due to historical inequities and discriminative practices. In general, APA guidelines suggest avoiding use of terms that can evoke stereotypic notions. Instead, be as specific as possible and avoid language that promotes stereotypic biases. In what follows, I take examples based on information in the American Psychological Association's online style guidelines (www.apastyle.org).

For example, when it comes to gender, unless you are specifically discussing an issue involving a man or a woman, you should avoid the use of gendered pronouns. Instead of writing "he" or "she," use "they" or "their" or try restructuring the sentence to remove the pronoun altogether.

For example, change a sentence like this:

> The doctor treated his patient with the latest drug.

to:

> The doctor treated the patient with the latest drug.

Avoid use of the term "mankind" and instead use "humankind," "people," or "humanity."

When writing about topics involving consideration of sexual orientation, care should be taken to be as specific as possible and avoid use of the label "homosexual." For example, change a sentence like this:

> The report detailed the discrimination faced by 100 homosexual couples.

to:

> The report detailed the discrimination faced by 60 gay male couples and 40 lesbian female couples.

In addition, do not confuse biological sex with gender roles. For example, do not write

> The sex of the participants had no effect on how they perceived the stimuli.

Instead write:

> The gender of the participants had no effect on how they perceived the stimuli.

Similarly, when describing people or participants, be as specific as possible about their race if race is relevant to the topic under consideration.

For example, in a paper about social stratification in India do not write:

> We interviewed a group of Indians.

India is a huge place with a great deal of racial, religious, and socio-economic diversity. Be specific:

> We interviewed a group of middle-class Sikhs from the Punjab region of northern India.

If describing the makeup of an experimental sample do not write:

> There were 20 White participants and 20 non-White participants in the sample.

Instead, be specific:

> There were 20 White participants, 10 Black participants and 10 Asian participants in the sample.

Note also that, in America, the term "African American" may be preferred over the word "Black." Be careful not to write so as to imply negative messages about race or ethnic origin.

For example, a sentence like this:

> The well-spoken Chinese professor gave a lecture.

could imply that Chinese professors are typically not well spoken. Instead simply write:

> The Chinese professor gave a lecture.

Finally, when referencing people with disabilities, put the person first. For example, replace this sentence:

> The disabled person was laughing.

with this one:

> The person with the disability was laughing.

Reporting Statistics

You should also be attentive to the APA's guidelines for the proper reporting of statistics. I will give just a couple of selected examples here.

Statistical values such as p-values should be placed in parentheses:

> The test revealed a significant effect of condition ($p=.032$).

Degrees of freedom should be placed in parentheses:

t-test: t (38)

ANOVA: F (2, 42)

Use an italicized N to refer to the total number of participants in the sample:

$N = 40$

Use a small italicized n to refer to number of participants in a particular sub-group of the sample:

$n = 20$

Formatting the Reference List

References are usually listed in alphabetical order, although some specific journals require numerical referencing instead. Most often, for students, alphabetical referencing is appropriate, but always check with your professor. When putting together the reference section at the end of your paper the basic APA format is as follows:

Blogs, J.F., Doe, J.M., & Silly, V.R.Y. (year). Title of paper. *Full journal title, volume*, start page–end page.

It is impossible for me to provide an exhaustive list of the style guidelines from the APA, so the onus is on you, the student, to study these guidelines and carefully implement them in your work. Remember, if in doubt, you can always approach your professor about the style that they require in written work.

Digital Object Identifier (DOI)

Over recent years it has become common to identify a record with a unique number known as the digital object identifier or DOI. When you access articles online, you can usually see the DOI included in the citation. The APA recommends that if such an identifier is available for the record you are citing, it should be included in your reference list, usually after the standard format reference.

Software Packages for Referencing

There are different software packages such as Refworks and Endnote that allow users to organize their references. They include the ability to create a reference list at the click of a button, in a particular style, such as APA style. If you have access to these types of software packages through your university library or department, I urge you to use them. They can save much time and effort and reduce the burden of making sure every comma and hyphen is in the right place. There are also apps and online formatting tools being developed all the time. A useful app for organizing papers on a Mac is called "Papers," and a quick Google search can direct you to websites that can take database record numbers (that accompany every paper listed in search results) to produce a citation in one of many possible formats. A quick Google search will also reveal numerous reference style convertors that people have programmed. For example, some may require that you input the Pubmed ID number of an article, and will then convert this to an APA style citation. I don't have a list of favourites to recommend for this type of reference conversion, but I encourage you to explore what's out there. Ask one of your university librarians about referencing resources that might be available through your university.

Proofreading and Editing

It should go without saying that you need to carefully proofread and edit your paper after you've written a decent first draft. When proofreading and editing, it is a good idea to give yourself a few days between finishing a draft and re-reading it. This helps ensure that you are coming to the draft with a "fresh" set of eyes. However, many students clearly do not engage in a thorough process of proofreading and editing. This is a huge reason for receiving a lower grade than could have been achieved, so I strongly urge you to take this stage of the process very seriously and give yourself time to read, edit, and re-read your work multiple times. A crucial thing to bear in mind when you're doing this is whether a non-specialist reader will be able to clearly follow your argument. Does each idea (paragraph) flow to the next? Or are there abrupt changes in focus that could benefit from improved transitioning? Do the points you make and the overall approach you have taken fit with what the professor was looking for? It is really important to consider this carefully. All too often, students write a brilliant paper, but completely miss the point that the professor was actually interested in. This is a failure of planning and often indicates that a student rushed to start a paper without fully considering what the professor is actually looking for. This underlines the importance of allowing yourself enough time to think about the process and about how you will do the best job possible.

Remember, at any point prior to the hand-in date, you can make an appointment with your professor and run your ideas by them to get an impression of whether you are on an appropriate track or not. Not enough students "use" their professors wisely! Professors are usually more than happy to talk with a student who demonstrates that they are really interested in the course and who has obviously done some thinking about the material and about what is required of them. More often than not, professors will go the extra mile to help such students. A common issue, however, is that a student goes to see a professor in a very unprepared state, having not thought about the issues at all. In this case, as I mentioned before, the student runs the risk of creating a bad impression. In addition, it is not a good idea to go to your professor the day before the deadline in a panic about your paper. The professor will not be impressed and indeed may not even have the time to speak with you at such short notice.

Finally, when editing and re-drafting, a useful technique is to imagine you received a bad grade and work through the paper to figure out why. This approach is helpful in enabling you to take a really critical look at what you have done and scrutinizing every aspect to see how it could have been written or laid out more effectively.

Lastly, as with presentations, it is always helpful to ask friends and family to read over your work, at least to determine whether the format is easy to follow. Very often we spend so much time on our own work that we lose perspective on which aspects are too specialized or too jargon filled. Despite our best efforts, it remains difficult to shake the curse of knowledge! It is not unusual for professors to draft and re-draft their own papers, grant applications, and other documents literally dozens of times, to try to "hit the right notes." Hence, one thing to bear in mind is that, once you've got your first draft, you really have only just started. In order to maximize your chances of getting an amazing grade, that draft will likely require considerable chopping and changing.

Plagiarism

Go to any university or college website and you will find a detailed discussion of plagiarism as it pertains to exams, assignments, lab reports, and virtually any piece of work you could be asked to do. In short, plagiarism is a very serious issue and the penalties for plagiarizing are harsh. Most universities consider plagiarism to be a serious example of academic misconduct. Given that plagiarism can be unintentional, it is important for students to fully understand what constitutes plagiarism and how to minimize their chances of, even accidently, plagiarizing in their work.

The Oxford dictionary defines plagiarism as the act of taking someone else's work or ideas and passing them off as one's own. Although this definition might imply that plagiarism requires a conscious attempt to "pass off someone else's work as your own," this is not the case. As alluded to above, even accidental or unintentional misuse of primary sources or failure to cite is considered plagiarism. My message for this section is simple: under no circumstances should you plagiarize intentionally, and you should be constantly on guard against plagiarizing by accident. Universities now routinely use sophisticated plagiarism detection software to check student papers for plagiarism.

Plagiarism doesn't just refer to direct cut-and-paste copying or handing in work done by someone else as your own. You are technically also plagiarizing if you simply paraphrase another source without citing it. One of the most popular plagiarism detecting software packages is called Turnitin. The developers of this software have identified 10 different forms of plagiarism ranging from the cut and paste variety to what they call the "aggregator" variety. This latter form of plagiarism involves the use of multiple sources and proper citation, but aggregated papers are problematic because they contain almost no original work (Turnitin white paper, available at http://turnitin.com/en_us/resources/white-papers). So, don't be fooled into thinking that plagiarism only refers to using work without citing it. It is more complex than that. For example, even if you change the words you've read in a primary source but retain the sentence structure, this is still considered plagiarism. Using quotations without quotation marks or a citation is considered plagiarism, and use of any of the "ghost writing" services found online is highly unethical and considered an especially bad form of plagiarism. Even recycling your own previous work and handing it in as a "different" assignment is considered "self-plagiarism" and is prohibited. Another situation in which plagiarism sometimes occurs is group-work scenarios. While it is perfectly acceptable for a group to use the same data, for example if the group ran a study together, the final write-up must be each person's own work (unless otherwise specified by the professor). When working in groups you need to be cognizant of even accidentally using other group members' work in your report.

You can minimize the chances of plagiarizing by simply citing the source for what you have written and ensuring that readers know where they can find the reference. However, as mentioned above, if the majority of your work is pulled from sources such that there is virtually no original contribution from you in your own work, this is still considered plagiarism. If in doubt about whether a particular approach constitutes plagiarism, you can always approach your instructor for guidance, or check with the appropriate office at your institution. At my home institution, the office that deals with issues of plagiarism is called the Office of Academic Integrity. Penalties for plagiarism vary depending on whether it's a first or repeat offence, the degree of plagiarism, and so on. For a first offence, the penalty could be a zero mark on the piece of work or a significant grade reduction. In addition, the offence can be registered with the Office of Academic Integrity, who may then carry out their own procedures involving a hearing of some kind in which the case is considered. The bottom line is, you don't want to be involved in a situation like this; it is harmful to your studies and your career prospects.

When all is said and done, and although it sounds clichéd, the only person that you are cheating if you choose to plagiarize is yourself. I strongly recommend that you study the information on your institution's website to fully understand what is considered plagiarism and work to ensure you don't plagiarize, even unintentionally.

In this chapter I've talked a lot about writing and have attempted to provide general advice that should be highly relevant no matter what kind of paper you are asked to write. When combined with the planning and time management techniques described in chapter 6, the advice given in this chapter can provide a powerful approach to the production of high-quality written work. But remember, good writing is a skill like any other, and the surest way to improve is to make sure you read other papers and books and practice writing at every opportunity. There are very few other situations where the old adage "practice makes perfect" is more appropriate. Happy writing!

Recommended Further Reading

American Psychological Association. (2010). *Publication manual of the American Psychological Association* (6th ed.). Washington, DC: APA.

Becker, H. S., & Richards, P. (2007). *Writing for social scientists: How to start and finish your thesis, book, or article.* Chicago, IL: University of Chicago Press.

Northey, M., Tepperman, L., & Albanese, P. (2012). *Making sense: A student's guide to research and writing: Social sciences,* fifth edition. New York, NY: Oxford University Press.

Pinker, S. (2014). *The sense of style: The thinking person's guide to writing in the 21st century.* New York, NY: Viking.

5
Group Work

Playing Well with Others: A Skill for Life

When you hear the term "group work," do you get excited or worried? You could be forgiven for experiencing either of these reactions because groups can be good or bad for learning. On the one hand, they can improve the educational experience, whereas on the other, depending on the makeup of the group, they can significantly worsen it. On the plus side, there is so much more that you as an individual student can learn when you work as part of a group; you gain access to the thoughts and insights of those around you, and each member of the group potentially benefits by getting "outside of their own head." Discussing ideas with others reduces reliance on your own expertise (or lack thereof) about a certain topic. It can be fun to throw around ideas with your group members and to essentially teach each other the concepts under consideration or correct each other's misunderstandings. In this way, group discussions facilitate the creation of ideas that no single group member could have come up with on their own, and the group can be considered greater than the sum of its parts. However, groups can slide from productive to unproductive pretty quickly. There's a "safety in numbers" kind of mentality that can be somewhat dangerous, like, for example, when some group members influence others to focus more on socializing and less on work (sound familiar?). This imbalance in focus has been the downfall of many a student group I've witnessed. This said, it is also true that not all groups are fun or indeed functional. It often only takes one person who is not a "team player" for the group dynamic to be ruined and for the experience to slide into a negative one.

Groups can be forums for conflict and strife. In one of the worst cases I've seen, I had a student working as part of an assigned pair who experienced anger and borderline threatening behaviour from their partner. Under such conditions, working with other people (or just another person) can become downright anxiety provoking, and even dangerous. The student in my class who informed me of her angry and "scary" partner had a very impressive attitude. To her credit, when she came to speak to me about the situation, she insisted that she was just informing me and didn't want me to take any action, or split up the pair. In my discussion with the student, she stated in a very mature manner that, in life, you can't always pick who you will end up working with, and that a key life skill is learning to get on with whoever you might be thrown in with, even if they are difficult, rude, or borderline threatening. I agreed with the first two points, but also said that I drew the line at "threatening." Despite me offering to reassign a partner, the student in question opted to continue on and navigate through the difficult partnership, using practical solutions such as meeting in public places instead of one-on-one in a private setting. Very impressively, she continued to work with her difficult partner and did a great job, despite the negative side of the experience. Overall, she left the class with a sense of achievement, not just at the good work she did, but also the life skills she felt she had developed. To be clear, don't think that you have to put up with bad behaviour from group members, as the student in the example did. If you are ever uncomfortable in a group work situation due to unacceptable behaviour from others, talk to your professor about it immediately to discuss potential solutions. While I've only ever had one experience like this, I've witnessed many dysfunctional groups and also many functional groups during my time running small group classes.

Seminars and tutorials are characterized by their smaller class sizes and a more interactive style, compared to larger lecture courses. Group work often takes the form of group presentations, but could also involve discussing course material or preparing for a debate, for example. In this chapter, I'll outline some ideas that will help you make the most of your group-work experience. First, you'll need to understand a bit about groups, and in particular, you'll need to be aware of some of the advantages and potential pitfalls of working in small groups.

Forming a Group

Regardless of the task your group is set, you will be expected to self-organize and work together to achieve it in an effective manner. In most seminar or tutorial situations, you will be assigned to a group by the professor, although in some cases, you may be allowed to pick your own group members. Usually groups consist of anywhere between three and six people. Members of a group are interconnected—that is the very nature of a group—but they do not necessarily start that way. When a group assembles for the first time, the dynamic has not been set, the individual members may or may not know one another, and the level of interconnectedness may seem low. How does the interconnectedness of a group manifest? What does it mean to be interconnected? Well, one way in which a group is interconnected can be appreciated by considering what happens if one group member is not a team player or has an antisocial, anti-productive manner. Even before the group develops cohesiveness or before group roles emerge, one "bad egg" can have a negative impact on everyone else. Sometimes, this situation is called the ripple effect—just as a pebble causes ripples when tossed into a pond, a single individual can have a widespread destructive effect on group functionality. I'll talk more later about strategies for dealing with unruly group members.

At the beginning of term, when I step in front of a seminar class or other small group class for the first time, there is always an air of nervousness and tension—ever so slight, but there. It can be felt even more strongly when I ask individuals in the group to introduce themselves to the rest of the group. Often people are hesitant to speak and there are long periods of silence, with some feelings of awkwardness. This is entirely normal and should not be taken as a sign that things are going badly. Communications researchers refer to this type of tension as "primary tension." They distinguish this from "secondary tension" which involves the inevitable social bumps and knocks that occur when members of the group interact to define their status and role within the group. Far from being a bad thing, this form of secondary tension can be healthy and actually help the group in considering new ideas or alternative ways of thinking. Of course, conflicts can occur, which, if not kept in check, can disrupt the group's affairs, but as long as the inevitable jockeying for position remains civil, secondary tension is nothing to worry about! You might ask how you can tell when tensions rise to the point where they become an issue. The answer to this is simple: if the group finds that it can no longer focus on what it is trying to achieve because the tensions are overwhelming, then the tensions have gone too far and the group must make an effort to get back on track before continuing on with the task at hand.

The Emergence of Roles in Newly Formed Groups

Once a group has assembled for the first time and each member has introduced themselves, there is a process of role emergence that tends to unfold. This is usually an organic process that develops with little deliberate effort, but it is important and worth thinking about. Roles can be thought of as behaviours that individuals are expected to engage in within a group context. Although role expectations may take some time to develop in a newly formed group, as the personal characteristics of the group members emerge, in certain predefined contexts, expectations are clear from the outset. For example, in a driving lesson, there is a clear role for the instructor: he or she is expected to teach the other person, the student, how to drive. By definition, then, the instructor will engage in behaviour that typifies someone telling someone else what to do. At times, this may even get volatile, such as when the student almost slams into the car in front or fails to check the rear-view mirror before changing lanes. Indeed, in such a situation, the instructor might even shout at the student.

Roles are fundamental within group contexts, and even randomly assigned arbitrary roles make a difference to how people behave and are perceived by others. A student who adopts a "teaching" style of behaviour may be perceived by others to be smarter than a student who is more passive and takes on a "learner" role in a group. This may not be true in fact, but just by virtue of the adopted role, perceptions of the people involved are affected. Assigned roles can also change the behaviour of individuals within a group. Perhaps the most famous case of this in psychological research was the Stanford prison experiments in which groups of students were randomly assigned to the role of prison guard or prisoner. Very quickly the guards began to harass and de-humanize the prisoners to such an extent that the first run of the experiment had to be stopped prematurely! Similarly, in group-work situations, if a student is assigned the role of leader, other students will look to them for direction, or if a student makes a joke and everyone laughs, they fall into the role of group clown. If a student doesn't say anything, they run the risk of being ignored. People adjust to emerging roles quite quickly and readily apply stereotyping. In many seminar and tutorial group-work scenarios, informal roles tend to emerge from the interactions of the group, and a student who takes on a leading role will receive implicit reactions from other group members which solidify or question their suitability for that role. One key to successful group work is for everyone in the group to take on a "we" and not an "I" focus. A group is nothing more than a collection of individuals if this critical focus on "we" is missing.

Generally speaking, researchers on group behaviour talk about three distinct types of roles that can be adopted. The first are *task roles* that help in moving the group forward toward their goal. The second are *maintenance roles* that help maintain the social harmony and cohesiveness of the group, and the third are *disruptive roles* in which individual needs are placed above those of the group—this can devastate group cohesion and productivity. The person who initiates and contributes a great deal is fulfilling a task role by offering lots of ideas, suggestions, and proposals. Similarly, task roles are also

performed by a "devil's advocate" who challenges the current thinking to force the group to reconsider their current position or by the
coordinating type of person who is good at pulling together different suggestions and points of view. People acting in maintenance
roles include individuals who are in tune with the feelings of other
group members and individuals who encourage the group and help
maintain feelings of togetherness. For example, someone playing a
maintenance role might bring cookies or donuts for everyone to
share at group meetings, or might try extra hard to coax the shyest
member of the group to speak out. These individuals are key to creating a harmonious atmosphere within the group. Finally, disruptive
roles are adopted by, for example, individuals who hog the limelight
by talking all the time and not letting others speak, individuals who
seem to get a kick out of opposing whatever the group consensus
seems to be, and individuals who constantly fight for control of the
group. I remember in one group I was a member of, there was one
person who would always throw a wrench in the works just as the
group was nearing a consensus on a topic of discussion. It was quite
infuriating for the other group members because all the progress
they thought they had made was suddenly undone, or at least set
back considerably. Individuals who fight for control of the group
can be difficult because they have an express desire to dominate the
group and are not particularly interested in working as a team or
letting others shine. They have a competitive as opposed to co-operative mindset and often interrupt and even disrespect other group
members.

Usually, in a newly formed group, individuals begin by playing the role they *want* to play (this is not necessarily based on
a conscious decision, but it can be). They might highlight their
strengths and showcase the skills they have to offer, or they might
be designated an initial role based on pre-existing stereotypes. For
example, in an all-male group with one female in it, the male
members of the group may expect the female member to take on
a more maintenance-related role, as opposed to being in the thick
of things with a leading task role. Again, this doesn't necessarily
happen consciously, but biases based on stereotypes can creep in
unbeknownst to the individual and can affect the way in which
the group develops. A key step in the formation of group roles

is the endorsement of the role any given member has adopted. For example, if Dave speaks up and attempts to play a leadership role in the first group meeting, but so does Raj, and group members see Raj's mastery over the subject matter to be better than Dave's, they may endorse Raj and not Dave for the role of leader. Endorsement can be a subtle process: people may not explicitly tell Dave they don't want him as leader, rather they may simply respond more favourably to Raj's input. A danger in role development in groups is when two or more individuals are vying for the same role and are unable to adjust their behaviour in accordance with the subtle feedback of the group. The adaptive thing to do, for any group member, is to accept the group's feedback; if that feedback does not represent an endorsement of the initial role the person has taken on, the individual should try to identify another role they'd like to play, until such a time that they receive endorsement from their peers. When individuals are not flexible, they can be very quickly labelled as "difficult"—and this can damage group cohesion. In their excellent book on effective teamwork, Larson and LaFasto (1989) highlighted three features of competent team members. First, a competent team member has skills that are relevant to the pursuit of the group's goal. Second, competent team members demonstrate a strong desire to contribute. They want to be a part of the group's activities and to have a role in achieving success. Third, competent team members are capable of collaborating with others. This collaborative mindset means leaving personal, selfish goals at the door and focusing on the group's shared goal(s). When you first get into a group situation, remembering these three key competencies will help you present yourself in a manner most efficacious to group success.

Top Tip

Roles emerge during the initial stages of group work. Rather than being rigid about the role you want to play, be flexible when it comes to taking on a role in a group. Inflexibility can lead to conflict, which is bad for the group. Always put the group ahead of the individual in group projects.

Everyone Wants to Play a Leading Role ... and if It's Done Right, They Can!

In a study of 16 groups working together for several weeks, it was found that about a third of groups did not have a leader come to the fore (Geier, 1967 cited in Rothwell, 2004). Interestingly, these groups were terrible both in terms of fulfilling their task objectives and in terms of social harmony. They were characterized by dysfunctional and frustrating interactions. In complete contrast, studies show that groups in which leaders do emerge and that developed stable member roles are generally successful. When the members of these 16 groups were interviewed, it is interesting to note that all but two of them expressed a desire to be a leader. Thus, the leadership role is much sought after, perhaps because of the status it affords and the ability it provides to exert influence over the direction taken by the group.

Very often, leaders of newly formed small groups emerge by a process of elimination. Research suggests that quiet members of the group are the first to be eliminated, followed by those who vocalize strong but unsubstantiated opinions, followed next by those that are not perceived to possess the required knowledge. The leader that eventually emerges is often the person with the best combination of task-specific and social skills, who is able to connect with the majority of group members. In general then, groups seem to endorse as leaders individuals who have a good blend of task-specific skills and social competence. In my own experience, the person who emerges as the leader is the person with excellent coordinative skills and a demonstrated willingness to put the time and effort into ensuring the group's success. They can communicate effectively with other members of the group and coordinate group activities in the service of the group goal. In happy, well-functioning groups, these individuals tend not to be autocratic, but are more like consultative facilitators.

Critically, an effective group leader helps bring out the best of their group members and can *share* the leadership role when appropriate. Maintaining leadership is a process drawn out over time. Usually, a leader emerges when the rest of the group indicates through their words or actions that they are willing to take on board the would-be leader's ideas, or at least are willing to perform task roles in a manner consistent with the suggestions of the leader. However, a would-be leader could be task competent and socially adept, but if the group does not respond to them favourably with a readiness to do what's needed, that person may not be the leader who eventually emerges.

One influential idea about effective leaders is that they are able to discern what the group needs at a particular time and step in to fill that role. For example, if Jane and Sarah are getting on each other's nerves during a discussion in an anthropology seminar group, John may see this, and step in to help them tone it down a bit. If later in the discussion the group asks a question about the lifestyle of a particular tribe in the Amazon jungle, John might realize this and quickly look this information up on his laptop and offer it up to the group to fill the need. Or, if three members of the group start offering their viewpoints and talking at the same time, John might calmly ask them to go one at a time—perhaps by inviting one of the group members to go first. This kind of "stepping in whenever there is a need" behaviour has been referred to by the term "leader as completer." Simply, a leader doesn't just set the agenda for meetings or find a meeting room and tell people what to do. Instead, they adapt to changing needs and step in to fill needs and gaps whenever they arise.

The preceding discussion might make it sound as if leadership is all about one person but this is not necessarily the case. As the title of this section says, everyone can play a leading role, but not by pushing each other aside in order to be the "boss." To be clear, I'm not advocating that multiple people co-lead a group, as research indicates that when left unchecked, this can lead to poor outcomes due to intragroup competition and a clash of egos. What I am advocating is that the person who emerges as the "organic" group leader creates an environment in which others can bring their leadership skills to the fore when appropriate. In this sense, leadership can be a multi-person affair. In fact the idea that only one person can lead can be destructive to the goals of the group when that leader doesn't empower others. So, when implemented correctly, leadership can and often should be shared. In the example given above, it didn't necessarily have to be John who kept stepping in when needs and gaps arose. Indeed, within a group work session, it is perfectly acceptable for various members of the group to lead by stepping in whenever they have the appropriate information or knowledge for the topic at hand. This is why successful companies have a chief marketing officer, a chief finance officer, and other specialist leaders. In this way, successful companies have co-operative *leadership teams*. On the smaller scale of student working groups, the in-tune group will afford each other the respect they deserve given the unique skills and knowledge they bring to the table. By allowing one another to step in when necessary, cohesion can be maintained, and the group becomes more effective. Such participative leadership is a common feature of well-functioning teams. Over the years, I have seen that often the person who ends up being the "leader of leaders" is the person who is willing to put the time into coordinating group activities and who has the social skills and abilities to "pull" the leadership qualities out of other group members. Thus effective leaders facilitate leadership in other team members and recognize when others know something better than they do. The effective leading person is often proactive and doesn't sit around waiting for someone else to organize the group's activities. Thus, a leader may emerge for various reasons within group work settings in tutorials and seminars, but if you want to play a leading role, essential skills include being proactive, hardworking, socially competent, willing to share leadership appropriately, and perhaps most importantly able to foster a co-operative climate.

Some students might worry that if someone else adopts the "boss" role, the professor will note this and they themselves will suffer correspondingly. This "zero-sum" view of the situation does not have to (and in fact, should not) prevail. The zero-sum viewpoint involves one member of the group feeling that they have failed just because another member does something well. The zero-sum mentality seems to suppose that there is only so much "reward" available and if someone else gets some of it, there'll be less for others. While this may be true in certain domains—for example there can only be one winner of the Olympic 100-metre sprint—this is a very unhealthy way to think about group work and can be completely destructive to successful group outcomes.

Again, a critical aspect of group success is to put "we" above "I." By respecting each other's strengths, group sessions can be structured so as to allow each member of the group to demonstrate their skills and therefore maximize their chances of being seen in a favourable light by any instructor who happens to be witnessing the interaction.

Bottom Line
Avoid a zero-sum mentality and work together! Avoiding zero-sum mindsets involves fostering co-operation and reducing competition within the group. It is fundamental to a group's success—if left unabated, competition can be devastating.

Group Ethos—Cooperate, Don't Compete

Our lives are full of competition and it is therefore not always easy to sweep aside the tendency to see any situation as competitive. At university, students compete for limited scholarships, for recognition from their professors and for a top GPA. In fact, the educational system is built on competition. The students with the best grades get the best scholarships and the positions in the best graduate schools or the best jobs after they've graduated. Competition is not just a factor in student life; the faculty members with the most publications and the biggest grants get the most recognition and often, in universities with merit pay systems, the most pay. Competition is so engrained in our society that it can easily become the default mindset in any situation. Nevertheless, competition is not always bad. It can be a great motivator and if done reasonably can encourage peers to strive to improve their own performance. However, within a group, competition can be toxic.

Research shows that despite its ubiquity in life, competition within a group does not create more functional and high-performing teams (Johnson & Johnson, 1989; 1998). On the contrary, research has found that co-operative groups do better than competitive groups. Thus, the idea introduced earlier seems to be true:

successful group functioning and performance necessitates a "we" and not an "I" orientation. One of the key factors in creating this advantage for co-operative teams relates to the idea of synergy. Synergy can be thought of as the idea that, "Together, we're greater than the sum of our parts." When teams work together, and use their unique skills in an integrated fashion, there is synergy. One person's weaknesses can be compensated for by another's strengths, and therefore the limitations inherent in any single member of the team can be overcome. In contrast, intragroup competition seems to promote the shielding of ideas and the withholding of information as opposed to information sharing. Not being able to share ideas and information is a tragic situation for a group that directly undermines performance. Thus, when you are put into a group, try to avoid the tendency to size up your group members in a competitive manner, and instead put effort into figuring out what each individual has to offer and how you can be a functioning, integrated team *together*.

So, it seems clear that co-operation trumps competition, but competition seems like a cultural norm that we take to different situations. When working in a group, how can we maximize the chances of creating a co-operative climate? Perhaps the most important thing for a co-operative group to have is a shared goal to work toward. Without such a goal to bind the efforts of group members together, it is hard to see how a group can emerge instead of a collection of individuals with their own personal goals. When first getting together as a group, it is therefore crucial to talk about what the group's goal is. What are you as a group trying to achieve? What does the professor want you to work on, and how will you be evaluated? Discussion of these aspects is fundamental to a good start to a group project and to fostering co-operation. In his excellent book on communicating in small groups, J. Dan Rothwell suggests a number of factors that are involved in facilitating co-operation. One of these factors is interdependence among group members. Five people sitting in a meeting room are not a co-operative group, but five people sitting in a meeting room working on a project with a shared goal are a group. The success of the group depends on the way in which the five individuals work together and depend on one another. Fostering a strong sense of this interdependence is a key element in creating a co-operative, high-functioning group. Essentially, a co-operative group is a group in which the members work together in a complementary fashion to achieve a shared goal.

Related to the concept of interdependence is the concept of accountability. If individual members of the group are depending on each other for the group's success, then they are also accountable to one another. Any failure to deliver by one person will affect the entire group's outcome. On a related note, a well-known problem within group contexts is social loafing—the tendency for some individuals to let others do the work while they benefit from the group's success. Clearly this is an unfair and unethical approach, but social loafing is rife. Social loafing can be discouraged by establishing expectations early on, for example with respect to attendance, preparedness, and contributions at group meetings. In extreme cases, the threat of being reported to the professor can also help "motivate" some social loafers, but this would be a last resort as there is likely to be a negative after-effect of such a course of action.

Another key aspect in forming co-operative groups is mutual encouragement to participate in interactions and conversations. This is a huge factor in groups and one that I see being neglected time and time again in my seminar groups. All group members should feel that their contributions are of value. All too often, one or two influential group members end up making all the decisions for the group. This situation is a real "contribution killer" and the more outspoken members of the group have a responsibility to encourage participation from the quieter members of the group in a non-token way. Without the contributions of the whole group you will miss out on the added value that comes from being part of a group process. To be clear, there is a difference between dividing up some work and then going off and doing it individually, and actually doing the work together as an interacting group. The creation of synergy is more likely in the latter case, and although it is always permissible for group members to have to do background work by themselves, the real added value of group work comes from the interactions between members. In this regard, each member of a group has a responsibility to encourage contributions from their team members. One way of helping quieter members of the group to contribute is to assign tasks to them. They may be too shy to outwardly request a role, but may respond very well to suggestions about which role(s) they might best fulfill in the group.

When working in a group, co-operation can be helped by each group member making a commitment to avoid directly criticizing or negatively evaluating the ideas of other group members. Effective interaction is fostered when each group member looks for the positive aspects of each contribution and treats other group members respectfully. Using a diplomatic approach and not ridiculing even far-fetched suggestions is nothing more than common courtesy. Avoid derogatory or accusatory language at all times. For example, don't throw blame around for setbacks and challenges that the group might face on its journey. By avoiding blame and accusation, you maximize the chances of fostering co-operation, not competition and conflict. Be straightforward but speak politely to avoid coming across as hostile. When communicating within your group, make effective use of body language. Just as I outlined in the chapter on delivering presentations, eye contact, body lean, and nodding serve as extremely powerful non-verbal cues that you are listening to what a fellow group member is saying. Subtly mimicking group members' speech or bodily movements can also increase feelings of rapport and friendliness. If you choose to employ mimicry, just be careful not to make it too obvious! Too much mimicry will likely be annoying and reduce rapport. Conversely, rolling your eyes or looking at another group member and giggling when someone is speaking is plain immature and does nothing to foster group cohesion. If you already know some of the other members when you come into the group situation, avoid the tendency to form cliques. Each group member should feel equal in the group, and favouring certain group members over others will only serve to splinter the team. Perhaps more subtle but still damaging to rapport is use of closed body language (folding arms, leaning back, turning away) while another group member talks. If you are truly interested in a successful group outcome, you need to make sure you put in every effort to make other group members feel like valued team members. Only then can you achieve the kinds of interdependence, accountability, and participation that effective groups need.

Structuring Group Meetings

So, we've seen that creating a co-operative group climate is paramount. But how does group work unfold? How do you actually get things done? It's important to be strategic and deliberate and use structure to foster progress in your sessions. After you've been assigned to a group, it's a good idea to have an initial meeting in which group members can introduce themselves and perhaps give their initial perspective on the topic under consideration. You might want to consider setting up an agenda to help you stay on topic and provide some structure. You can create an email list for your group and send the agenda out at least a week before the first meeting. This requires someone to step up and take responsibility for kick-starting the process. An agenda for the first session can be simple and might look something like this:

Agenda for discussion of our project:
The link between education and crime in the US

Date: XX/YY/ZZ
Location: Meeting room 1
Time: 6-8pm

Purpose: Introductions and discussion about how to tackle this project

i. Introductions
   a. Please prepare a short intro including your academic background and key strengths—i.e., are you good at statistics, writing, etc?
   b. As well as the academic stuff, please provide one or two fun facts about yourself so the rest of the group can get to know you!

ii. Open discussion
   a. What is the scope and end-goal of this project, and what does doing this well constitute?
   b. How do we best achieve this goal together?
   c. When and how often should we meet?
   d. Any other issues?

iii. Actions before next meeting
   a. What should each one of us do between now and next meeting?

iv. Any other business

v. Adjournment—head out for pizza?

Figure 5.1   Sample Agenda

One idea that might be useful is to keep minutes of the meetings your group holds. Minutes are essentially a succinct written description of the meeting with an indication of who said what and a general record of what was discussed. In certain situations it might be appropriate to submit these minutes as supplementary information to your professor so they can see for themselves just how organized and effective your group's approach to the work was. Of course, your professor may not be willing to look at this extra material, in which case the minutes could still be useful for group members to remember what was said and what decisions were made, for example if tasks were assigned to various people. In the event of a group member being unexpectedly absent, the minutes can keep them in the loop.

It's perfectly acceptable to list an agenda item as "open discussion" although it's very helpful to jot down a few pointers for what the group can actually discuss. In many cases, even a simple structuring like this can massively increase efficiency and productivity for group projects. However, when it comes to problem solving in groups, there are even more specific ideas that have emerged through research over the years.

One structured approach to problem solving that has proven to be very effective consists of six stages and has emerged out of the extensive work on human problem solving and in particular the "reflective thinking model" of philosopher and educator John Dewey (Dewey, 1910, cited in Rothwell, 2004). Dewey wrote an influential book called *How we think* in which he outlined a set of steps that a rational individual should traverse when confronted with a problem. These steps are often referred to as "the Standard Agenda." The stages, along with a brief description of what each stage involves, are listed below.

1. *Problem identification stage.* This stage involves a serious consideration of what you have been asked to do. What exactly is the problem at hand? This stage can also be considered the goal-formulation stage. The group should focus on clearly defining the goal they are seeking to achieve.

2. *Problem analysis stage.* During this stage, the group collects information about the problem, thinks about the problem

from different angles, and discusses the various ways in which the problem can be conceived.

3. *Solution criteria stage.* This stage involves figuring out what a successful solution to the problem must look like. It doesn't require figuring out solutions, but the criteria by which an effective solution would be identified and judged. You might consider what the professor has stated you need to demonstrate with the project as part of this process.

4. *Solution suggestions stage.* This is a brainstorming process during which individual group members "empty their heads" of all potential solutions, even ridiculous ones. Brainstorming is characterized by a lack of editing and the use of some kind of representational format like a whiteboard, computer-based mind map, or audio recording. Sorting and triaging can be done after the initial brainstorming session.

5. *Solution evaluation and selection stage.* Here, the possible solutions identified in the previous stage are evaluated in the light of the criteria discussed in stage 3. Which possible solutions fulfill the criteria?

6. *Solution implementation stage.* Producing the final product that will be used in the next piece of work the group is going to do. In a seminar or tutorial this could be a group presentation, or other group assignment of some kind. All the preceding stages are practically useless if this stage is not completed well!

Of course, these are *guidelines* and should be thought of as such—not as black and white rules. It is not necessarily easy to perform each stage of this process without some strife. For example, achieving consensus in groups can be notoriously difficult. Do you vote on different possible solutions? What if the group is split 50/50? There is no magic formula for resolving these kinds of issues. The hope is that some structure and a systematic approach can make group work more efficient and more fulfilling. In the 50/50 split opinion case, a true test of the group is the ability for each opinion holder to justify why they hold their opinion and convince the rest of the group that it is the right opinion under the circumstances. If nothing else, going through this process will improve everyone's ability to make their case in the strongest possible way.

Common Pitfalls of Group Thought and Decision Making

So far, we've highlighted that member roles often emerge organically in groups and that groups should be co-operative, should share leadership when appropriate, and should implement structure so as to maximize efficiency and productivity. A quick note is in order regarding the notion of member roles. Although it is useful for each group member to be aware of the functional role they play in the group, do not fall into the trap of thinking that roles are set in stone. It is perfectly possible for roles to be "renegotiated" or for goals to flexibly change during the deliberations of the group. For example, if someone has been a key direction giver during early deliberations, but it becomes clear that the purpose of the group's activity is evolving, that particular direction giver may end up becoming more of a follower or implementer. What this actually means is that people often cycle through roles in a group over time. In fact, in many organized groups, this cycling through roles is built in to the system. For example, most university departments have a chairperson, who is a faculty member in the department, but who is replaced by another faculty member from the department after some time.

I mentioned right at the beginning of the chapter that groups can be good or bad. Groups can be good because they offer an unprecedented opportunity to learn from one another and to experience synergy—a whole experience that is greater than the sum of the individual parts. However, being in a group can have its downsides. Some common biases that affect individuals can be present in groups as well, and can even be magnified. This can end up causing the group to draw incorrect conclusions that can be devastating to the group's performance and ultimately their grade for the project! In a sense, groups can sometimes fall prey to a sort of mindlessness that can really hamper effective problem solving. An obvious issue in a group comprising several non-invested members is diffusion of responsibility and social loafing. Diffusion of responsibility simply refers to falling into the trap of thinking that someone else will step up. Social loafing can occur when an individual reaps the rewards of the group, without pulling their own weight. Over and above these common issues, there are a few common biases that can affect groups. In the remainder of this section I'll outline them with the hope that, if they are on your radar, you can remain vigilant and guard against them.

Often a group will be involved in trying to figure out something or come to a conclusion based on information they have researched and collated. This process of using known information to inform a question whose answer is unknown is open to all sorts of inferential errors. Inference can be thought of as the act of forming an opinion on the basis of known information. To a large extent a successful outcome of a group task is dependent on the quality of the inferences that the group makes based on the information it has accumulated. It is easy to see then, that if the information is poor, of low quality, or insufficient, inferences can be wrong. A key aspect of this potential problem is that evaluating information is not an easy thing to do. A very frequent mistake that people make is not differentiating between correlation and causation. In most undergraduate statistics classes the notion that "correlation is not causation" is repeated mantra-like, but so strong is our tendency to make this error that we remain susceptible. For example, if you just bought yourself a new set of running shoes, let's say the fanciest, most expensive pair on the market, with new technology in the soles, and then you go out and run your fastest five kilometres ever, it would be tempting to conclude that the new technology in the shoes were causal in your performance. However, this could be wrong. Perhaps you were just excited and motivated to run fast because you love your new shoes, or perhaps you had a good night's sleep and good nutrition before the run. You must always take care when evaluating information not to make this most common of mistakes. One wrong causal statement can cascade when other members of the group unthinkingly agree with the person making the inference. You can easily imagine how one bad inference built on another can be disastrous.

In addition to wrongly assigning causal relationships, human beings also have a tendency to give a lot of weight to highly emotional, easy-to-visualize information and rather less weight to less emotive information. For example, when news of a terrible airplane crash emerges, individuals are strongly influenced by this news when thinking about the risks involved with flying. This may occur despite the fact that statistics show flying to be among the safest forms of travel. When drawing a subsequent conclusion about the danger of flying, individuals must be on guard against giving too much weight to a highly emotive, vivid example of a disaster. Another issue that can reduce the quality of inferences made is not doing deep or extensive enough research to find representative information about an issue. For example, if you are researching the potential link between diets high in red meat and cancer and you find two papers indicating that the correlation is non-existent, you might conclude that studies show no correlation. However, if you had done a more extensive search, you may have found 25 other papers that revealed a link, and without incorporating this information you run the risk of basing your conclusion on an unrepresentative piece of information.

Bottom Line

A little knowledge is a dangerous thing. Invest time to do comprehensive information searches to avoid falling prey to reliance on unrepresentative information. In group settings, one bad piece of information can easily lead to a cascade of bad inferences.

Another strong human tendency is to search for and pay a great deal of attention to information that fits with our pre-existing assumptions and ideas about a particular issue or topic. For example, someone that holds the stereotype that African Americans are criminals may be more likely to pay attention to news stories or media depictions involving crimes committed by African Americans, and may fail to pay equivalent attention to stories involving crimes committed by white Americans. This notion that human beings tend to pay more attention to information that confirms their pre-existing ideas is called the confirmation bias and it is one of the strongest biases that we as humans display.

Bottom Line
Be mindful of the confirmation bias and step back from the situation to reflect on whether you or anyone else in your group is falling prey to the confirmaation bias.

A friend of mine once came out with a joke that relates to another human tendency that can be problematic. He said, "There are two types of people in this world, those who dichotomize and those who don't!" The Oxford dictionary defines "dichotomize" as to divide into two parts, classes, or groups. In my opinion, the tendency to dichotomize is one of the worst, most prevalent problems among even seasoned researchers in the social sciences. Cognitively, it may be easier to divide the world into groups of two: there are criminals and law-abiding citizens, there are healthy people and unhealthy people, there are rude people and polite people, there is the correct theory and the incorrect theory, and so on. In each of these easily stated groupings, even a few seconds of thought reveals that there are possibilities that exist outside of the two groupings. Even a largely law-abiding citizen can break the law, whether it's occasional speeding or illegally downloading music or movies. Likewise, even the most polite person can be rude under certain circumstances and even a healthy person can have health problems or be unhealthy sometimes. The failure to see the whole possibility space outside of extreme alternatives can lead people to ignore information that might be highly pertinent to the issue at hand. When making detailed deliberations about a topic, the nuances are often what are most interesting, and the tendency to dichotomize can steer you away from the nuances.

Finally, to round out this section on common issues, you may have heard the term "groupthink." Groupthink refers to a phenomenon

Bottom Line
Remember the richness of possibilities; there are usually more than two!

whereby members of a group, not wanting to disagree with other members, start to agree with statements and ideas that are wrong. This tendency can be increased in situations where individuals want to avoid being labelled as troublemakers or do not want to show their disagreement for political reasons. For example, imagine in a sociology class on deviance you're part of a group discussing why America has more gun crime than Canada. Suppose further that one of your group members is from America and is a few years older than everyone else in the group. In this example, let's imagine that they offered up a reason as follows: "I saw this documentary on YouTube a couple of years back and it said that the reason there's more gun crime in America has nothing to do with the number of guns per capita. It's actually because there are more immigrants from third world countries in the US, and for these immigrants, using guns to settle disputes is normal. Canadian immigration is better controlled, so that's why Canada doesn't get the gun crime." Having made this totally wrong claim based on a YouTube video they supposedly watched, a couple of people in the group look at each other, with a strong sense that they both recognize that the opinion given is wrong. However, the group has been functioning really well and everyone likes each other, and the older student from America has been a pretty good and well-intentioned contributor so far. After a few seconds the group members realize that no one else in the group is countering the claim, and, not wanting to rock the boat, not a single person disagrees. What's happening in this example is classic groupthink. To maintain group cohesion, the issue is not talked out as it should be, and an incorrect idea is accepted when it clearly shouldn't be. This is precisely what groupthink entails: maintaining group cohesion, out of fear of disagreement and conflict, but at the expense of clear, well-evidenced thinking.

Bottom Line

To avoid groupthink it behooves every group member to think critically about what is being suggested and for the group to explicitly outline, maybe in the first meeting, that challenges to groupthink will be encouraged and not looked upon unfavourably.

Conflict in Groups and Working with Difficult Group Members

Unfortunately, working in groups is not always plain sailing. There are sometimes issues involving a difficult group member, or with group members working against each other as opposed to with each other in the pursuit of the group's goals. Conflict is usually thought of as a strong disagreement that results in arguments and potentially even anger. However, not all conflict is bad—conflict can be constructive in the sense that, in a well-functioning group in which members respect each other's input, disagreements can open up new possibilities of thought. This is only possible when the involved parties are open and flexible. Being open and flexible helps group members to work through any differences and find a mutually agreeable solution. Some might call this a compromise, in which differing views are partially given up for the good of the group's progress. Constructive conflict can only really occur in a group that has adopted a co-operative as opposed to a competitive climate. Much more often though, we talk about conflict being destructive, as is the case when group members are inflexible, closed to the opinions of others, defensive about their own opinions, and competitive. Effective leadership on the part of other group members is good for managing conflicts. Recall that we described qualities of an emergent leader as involving both task-specific abilities and *social competence*. Social competence allows individuals to build and not burn bridges with other members of the group. If a conflict arises within a group, it may be useful to explicitly confront the fact that it's there. Basically, this can be thought of as "calling it" and can be really helpful in situations where, for example, two members of the group have been taking verbal jabs at each other. By bringing this situation out into the open you encourage the parties to fix it, or risk taking the group off the rails. The successful conflict manager then works to try to move the parties closer to agreement by getting them to spell out what their concerns or gripes are and then suggesting solutions that at least address the most important issues. In the real world, it's likely impossible to get the parties to agree on everything, so a useful approach is to identify the most significant concerns and focus on those and get the parties to forget about any minor issues. Just clearly stating the issues when a conflict arises is often enough to figure out common ground. Many conflicts are built on a misunderstanding of the other person's position. Another extremely important part of resolving conflict is for non-involved members of the group to help calm the involved parties down. Having a group member focus on this important maintenance task is crucial to help de-escalate a conflict.

If one of your group members becomes angry, it's important not to respond to them in an angry tone but rather to respond in a calm and soothing manner. This is sometimes referred to as an asymmetrical response. You should acknowledge that the angry person has a point and that people are receptive to hearing them out. You might also request them (calmly) to reiterate why they're upset and encourage them to describe in detail what the issue is. This is often enough to make an angry, venting person realize that the group is interested in what they have to say, and to get them to start to say it in a non-confrontational way. However, under no circumstances should any group member stand for being verbally (or in extreme cases physically) abused. There are "lines" that correspond to what we would find acceptable in everyday life. Everyone knows these lines and group members must use common sense to determine when a line has been crossed. Under such circumstances, the same options are available to the victim of abuse as would be available in any other situation, and include campus security, police, or other support services.

Before it ever gets to this, though, take time to set expectations from the outset. I am a strong believer in setting expectations *early on* when embarking on group work. If, during the first one or two group meetings, the group explicitly discusses potential issues such as angry or offensive outbursts, social loafing, and competitiveness, and defines them as unacceptable, many of these most common problems for groups can be avoided. Getting buy-in early on regarding acceptable norms for behaviour within the group and pre-empting potential problems can be a very smart way to make sure your group remains functional, happy, and ultimately productive!

A Quick Word about Culture

With increasing globalization comes the strong possibility that you will have students from other countries and cultures in your seminar or tutorial class. In particular, most universities in North America and Europe are seeing increasing enrollments from students of Asian origin, principally coming from China. It's important to be sensitive to cultural differences when interacting in groups. For example, many individuals from Asian cultures have what cultural psychologists refer to as "a collectivist orientation"—that is, the group is generally prioritized over the individual. In Western culture however, an "individualistic orientation" tends to dominate such that the individual is prioritized over the group. There are potential pitfalls with both orientations and it's important to realize this distinction between cultures. It is also important to realize that this distinction is a generalization. That is, there are individuals with both orientation types (collectivist, individualist) in both cultures. In general though, excessive individualism can work against a "we" identity for the group, whereas an excessive collectivism can result in too much conformity and potentially contribute to problems such as groupthink. That is, a collectivist, out of concern for not going against the group may not voice an important concern that could help stop the group from making bad inferences. Indeed, in some Asian cultures, what North Americans and Western Europeans would consider assertiveness is sometimes considered as disruptive behaviour and disrespectful to others. On top of this, the fact that English language ability may differ between domestic and foreign students adds another level of complexity. It is important that *all* group members, regardless of their status as a domestic or foreign student (or a female or a male, or an ethnic minority or a member of the majority for that matter), are encouraged to contribute by the rest of the group. Remember, just because someone is not talking all the time, it doesn't mean they've got nothing to say! In my opinion, the increasingly multicultural makeup of our universities is a great thing. The different perspectives that people bring can fuel the creation of solutions to a problem that would not be possible without the insight from a member of another culture. Learning to function effectively in multicultural groups is also a key transferrable skill that will likely serve you well after you graduate and enter the workforce. See diversity within a group as a strength and not a weakness.

Recommended Further Reading

Burtis, J. & Turman, P. (2006). *Group communication pitfalls*. Thousand Oaks, CA: Sage Publications.

Esser, J. (1998). Alive and well after 25 years: A review of Groupthink research. *Organizational Behavior and Human Decision Processes, 73*, 116–141.

Johnson, D. & Johnson, R. (2009). An educational psychology success story: Social interdependence theory and co-operative learning. *Education and Educational Research, 38*, 365–379.

Larson, C.E. & LaFasto, F.M. (1989). *Team Work: What must go right/what can go wrong*. Newbury Park, CA: Sage Publications.

Rothwell, J.D. (2004). *In mixed company: Communicating in small groups and teams* (5th ed.). Belmont, CA: Wadsworth.

6

Planning and Time Management

Time Never Comes Back: Plan to Use It Effectively!

When I was growing up I used to love hanging out in the back garden of our home; it was a place of fun and games and also quite a bit of pondering. My dad was a keen golfer and his golf bag was usually in the trunk of the car. One of my favourite things to do was take a club from his golf bag and chip golf balls in the garden. I could do this for hours at a time. During the pacing between rounds of chipping, I used to think and talk out loud to myself about whatever was on my mind, including pending school work. Around exam time, or in the lead-up to an important assignment, rather than putting the golf club away and heading indoors to "focus," I found myself in the garden more than usual. At one point, my mom, thinking that I was procrastinating a little too much, suggested that I quit messing around in the garden, get inside, and get to work. But for some reason I didn't operate that way, and any attempts to standardize my approach at my desk just didn't yield the same kind of creative thinking that I managed to conjure up chipping golf balls in the garden. I found that chipping in the back garden was an extremely useful time for sorting my thoughts and preparing myself to start a project. I didn't realize it at the time, but my approach was not necessarily bad, despite the conventional wisdom at the time that work was done at a desk. Chipping, pacing, and thinking was my unique style, and it seemed to work. Although I wasn't a stellar student in high school, I wasn't bad and I got things done to a level that enabled me to eventually go on to university and discover my real passions.

I notice that even now as a university professor, I spend many hours thinking about current and future projects away from my desk (most professors probably do; we're obsessed). Often I'll do this while walking around campus, or if I'm home, while walking around the neighbourhood. Why am I telling you this? The point here is that we are all unique individuals with our own individual approach to life and work. Sometimes, we need an overhaul in how we approach, plan, and execute work, but only if the approach we are currently using doesn't get the job done. Far too often I see books prescribing the "best" way to manage time and espousing a one-size-fits-all solution. For students of seminars and tutorials, planning, scheduling, and executing work—whether it's preparation for a presentation or a research proposal—happens within the overall context of their university workload and personal commitments. In this chapter, I'll review some popular ideas about planning and time management, but I won't take a prescriptive approach. Instead, I offer my thoughts around common strategies and leave it to you to think about whether any of these ideas might work for your unique personal style.

A Quick Preview

Before we get into the details of planning and time management, here's a quick preview of what I'll talk about in the rest of this chapter. When you read the plethora of time management and productivity books, you realize that many of them include an approach that can be boiled down to five basic steps. The first step is to identify what you stand for as a person and to identify your goals going forward. The second step is to create specific project or task lists, which include details of specific actions needed to complete those tasks. Completing these actions will help move you closer to your goals. The third step involves the prioritization and actual scheduling of these tasks and actions. The fourth step is the most critical—this planning is useless unless you execute the required actions. This is vital, or you will not move closer to your desired outcomes. To ensure that your approach is sustainable and doesn't fall by the wayside, a fifth step is crucial: you must review and update your lists regularly and in detail. In the bulk of the rest of this chapter I'll detail each stage of this process and I'll take a few detours to discuss related issues along the way. Much of what I cover in this chapter is inspired by classic time management strategies such as those espoused by David Allen in his popular book *Getting things done*. For anyone wishing to delve deeper into Allen's ideas, I strongly recommend reading his book—in my opinion it is one of the best such guides out there, and implementing the strategies he suggests will almost certainly make you more efficient. You can find more information about Allen's approach at his website (www.gettingthingsdone.com).

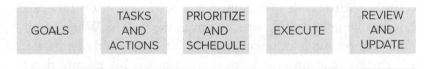

Figure 6.1   Five Essential Components to Effective Planning and Productivity

Knowing Yourself and Defining Your Goals

Once I heard an analogy of life as a boat making a journey across the sea. It made me think, so I'll share it. The sea can be a rough place for a boat, and if it loses its sail or its motor, it becomes a hostage to the water and weather, drifting this way and that, without advancing toward its destination. As soon as the sail or motor starts working again, the boat is no longer at the mercy of the sea. With a functioning motor, the influence of sea currents can be somewhat overcome. In this way, a boat with an intact sail or motor can move toward its destination in a relatively controlled fashion, dealing with the perturbations imposed by currents and weather. Importantly, such a boat can also change its course and take an alternative route, or even pick a new destination entirely. When you think about yourself, are you more like a boat with a broken motor, being pushed around by external forces, or are you using your motor appropriately to help get to where you need to be? Put another way, do you feel a high level of control over how your life is unfolding, or is your life unfolding in a way that is *completely* dependent on external forces?

Thinking about yourself as a boat trying to get from A to B might be a useful analogy for envisioning your journey through university. You are a student, trying to graduate and then move on to the next big thing in the journey of life. Even if you don't know exactly what your next big thing in life is (also known as what you want to be "when you grow up"), you know that you will be best positioned if you focus on developing as many skills as you can, and graduating with a solid GPA.

To be a successful university student, you need to be able to complete your work to a high standard, hand it in on time, and (ideally) avoid becoming stressed out in the process. When beginning your planning for organizing your life, it is useful to start with a high-level exercise that helps sketch out the big picture that is your life.

The Preparatory Step to Getting Organized: Knowing Yourself

In modern society, most people have various roles in different areas of their lives. They might be a student at university, a sibling and a daughter within a family, a significant other in a romantic relationship, an employee in a workplace, an athlete on a sports team, and so on. Many productivity gurus suggest that the first thing you need to do when planning for a productive life is to take a broad overview of your life as it stands and figure out, for each part of your life, where you are heading. Put another way, for each facet of your life, what are your goals?

Before you answer this question, though, there's another useful step. Take a few moments or many moments to have a think about the kind of person you are or want to be. What do you stand for as an individual—what do you value? A useful exercise is to list all the values or qualities that a person could strive for and then create a list of your top five or ten values and try to prioritize them. This process is similar to what some businesses do when they create vision and mission statements. They try to identify what their core values are and then use those values to guide the development of their vision and mission statements so as to make sure their business practices line up with their core values and don't work against them.

As an individual, you might identify honesty, hard work, a sense of humour, humility, compassion, open-mindedness, sincerity, leadership, helpfulness, and fairness as your top ten guiding values. You might then whittle this list of ten down to any combination of five values. The idea is that, in everything you do in life, you let these values guide you; if you are ever at a point where a potential goal or action conflicts with one of these core values, you would modify that goal or action accordingly so that you stay true to your core values. This exercise to identify core values is extremely useful to make explicit what you are about as a person. It's amazing how having a clear idea of this can help when confronted with the vast number of choices you are presented with at university. Many of us have values held at a subconscious level but we don't think about them explicitly very often; reminding yourself of them increases their salience and can be helpful. Once you have identified your top few core values, ask yourself honestly what you are doing to practice, promote, and live by these values.

Defining Your Goals

Once you've consciously pondered your personal values, you can move onto thinking about your goals for the future. A popular technique is to divide your life up into areas or domains and determine what you want to achieve in each area in the next few years, or at least the next year. Some people insist that having a 10-year goal is necessary, and I think for some aspects of life this might be true. But for a typical student, I don't think having a 10-year goal is critical. I do believe, however, that having a clear idea of what you want to achieve in the next one year is absolutely crucial for successful planning and time management. If you can manage to identify where you'd like to be in two, three, four, or five years, even better, but if not, don't sweat it. When it comes to the importance of setting long-term goals it's very simple: if you don't know where you are heading, how do you decide what activities to allocate your time to in the coming days, weeks, and months?

From Long-Term Goals to Concrete Actions

Once you've set your goals, you need to figure out how to break these down into component tasks, which themselves may consist of many actions. You may have identified areas of your life as "university/work," "personal/family," "spiritual," and "health and fitness." For each area identify one or two important long-term goals that reflect what you want to achieve in the next one to five years. This can be very difficult—even setting goals for next month can be tricky sometimes, so you'll have to think hard about it, and don't forget to be led in your thinking by your core values! The first stage is to think generally about what you want to achieve. As a third-year undergraduate student you might say something like "In five years I want to be in a good graduate school for psychology, well on my way to getting my PhD." One of your health and fitness goals over a shorter time period might be "I want to run a half-marathon next summer, and then a full marathon one year after that" or "I want to become proficient in yoga and make sure I'm practicing at least three times per week within six months." A spiritual goal might be "Within the next six months I want to learn to meditate, and practice for 10 minutes every morning." Notice that these goals are (relatively) specific. You could have said, "I want to go to graduate school," instead of "a good graduate school in psychology." The extant research on goal setting suggests that being specific when you set goals results in better performance than being vague. So, try to be as specific as possible when doing this exercise. Another interesting aspect of goal setting pertains to whether you specify a performance level as your goal (such as, "get an A+" in a course) or whether you specify a "mastery goal" instead. Mastery goals focus more on improvement than attaining a specific performance level, and there is some evidence that such goals can improve self-efficacy and lead to more successful goal pursuit.

The next part of the process is to ask yourself what you need to do to maximize the chances of making these desired achievements a reality. You might break down the five-year university goal stated in the preceding paragraph into three shorter-term goals for next term:

1. I need to pick a majority of research-oriented courses, make sure I learn core principles of psychological research, and aim for an A+ in these courses.
2. I need to research and identify the best graduate schools for psychology.
3. I need to obtain a research assistant position in a lab to gain hands-on research experience.

You can dig down more and identify specific steps required to help you with point 1 above:

1. Research and select courses which are most pertinent to psychology research training and register for them.
2. For each course, communicate with professor and TA to understand what they expect for each type of assessment in the course, and try to get a sense of what is required to get an A+ in the course.
3. For each project or assignment, establish a workflow process that will help get the work done to a high standard and in time.

You can whittle this latest list down even further into specific actions that you'll need to take. For example, for point 2 in the preceding list you might identify a concrete action step as:

Specific action for item 2 on preceding list: *Go to department website and find contact information for professors who teach the courses I've selected for next term; make a contact list.*

You can do a similar exercise for each of your longer-term goals. This way, at the end of this planning exercise, you at least have a feel for your core values, your goals for the next year at least, the steps involved in moving you toward your goals and the specific actions you need to take.

To be sure, this process will take time when you initially do it. But, it is highly useful for organizing your life. When you go through this process, be sure to adopt the much talked about **SMART** approach to setting your goals. This approach recommends that goals should be **S**pecific (research shows that specific goals lead to better performance than vague goals), **M**easurable (how you will know when you've achieved a particular goal), **A**ttainable (research shows that goals should be difficult but achievable and certainly not too easy), **R**ealistic (making a goal unrealistic can de-motivate you when you don't see progress toward it) and **T**ime-based (knowing when you need to achieve an outcome by is critical).

Once you have generated lists of long-term (for example, one year) goals, as well as the intermediate shorter-term goals and next actions that will help get you there, it is imperative not to forget about them. This may sound obvious, but it is quite common to spend lots of time and effort making lists of goals before slowly but surely letting them slip off the radar. Perhaps the best example of this situation are New Year's resolutions. Research shows that less than 50 per cent of resolvers reported continuous success after six months (Norcross, Mrykalo, & Blagys, 2002). So how can you ensure that you stick with the program and use your time in the service of your goals? I'll talk more about reviewing your action lists later in the chapter, but it is also imperative to keep your overall goals in mind (both long and short term). One obvious tactic to help with this is to make sure your keep your goals close at hand so you can refer to them often. When you see things often, you internalize them and you can then more effectively keep them at the forefront of your mind. Keeping goals fresh in mind also serves to motivate you and remind yourself about the big picture of why you are doing what you are doing. Thus, you should look over and review your goals weekly, monthly, and yearly. Weekly reviews can help you keep track of progress toward short-term goals, whereas monthly reviews can help track your progress toward longer-term goals. When you look over your goal list, you can determine whether you are getting closer to achieving them, further away from achieving them, or whether you are stagnant. You can then tweak your project list and specific action plans and adjust your priorities to maximize your chances of moving toward your goals. In some cases, this monitoring can even help you realize that what you thought was an important goal is actually not that important after all. Goals can be changed as your ideas and aspirations in life evolve.

One method to keep on track and motivate yourself involves estimating a "distance from goal" when you do your monthly review. The idea is to make a table in which one column lists your goals and another column lists a percentage or other numeric estimate that represents how far along the path to the goal you are. Of course, you must try to give an honest assessment of where you are with respect to the goal in question (self-deception is not particularly helpful when thinking about meeting goals). If the goals you've set are actually measurable (the "M" in SMART), then you should be able to quantify your current state and come up with some idea about how far it is from your desired state. Although this approach of "discrepancy reduction" is very easy when goals involve precise numbers such as how much you weigh or assignment grades over time, it can be harder with less tangible goals. This is part of the reason to think hard about making goals measurable. Having said this, I think it is possible to estimate current status even with less precisely measurable outcomes or goals.

Thinking regularly about progress toward your goals is helpful because when you can see a trend that you're moving in the right direction, you won't want to jeopardize things by doing things that won't help you get closer to the goal in question. Conversely, if you see that you are moving further away from your goal over time, it may be a signal that your goal was too unrealistic or that your motivation to achieve it has dwindled. At this point, reconsidering or reframing your goal is a great way to get yourself back on track. Another aspect of goal setting that research has shown to be effective is a public commitment to goals. The idea is that, by telling someone else about your commitment to your goal(s), you feel more accountable, which in turn has a motivating effect. Finally, when you review your progress and realize that you are actually inching closer to your desired outcome(s), this increases your self-belief that you can achieve your desired performance levels, which in turn motivates you to stick with your plan.

So far, we've talked about goal setting and breaking longer-term goals into shorter-term goals and specific next actions. We haven't really discussed how you schedule your work, how you ensure that you can keep track of the projects you have to do, and how you make sure you actually do the work that needs doing. In the next sections, we focus more specifically on the situation that you will face as a seminar or tutorial student.

The Pitfalls of To-Do Lists

In the preceding sections, it's obvious that lists are an important part of effective planning. You made lists of goals, sub-lists of shorter-term goals and tasks, and lists of specific actions. Since lists seem to be key, let's think about them for a minute. Do you make lists? Many people do and many people find them incredibly helpful for organizing their lives. But think for a minute. What does your to-do list usually look like? Do you have a daily to-do list in your calendar? Perhaps you're super well intentioned and every morning over a coffee, you painstakingly construct the list of things you have to do today and maybe even the exact time slots on your calendar when you'll get them done. If you're lucky, this works for you and you don't need to worry about overhauling your planning and time management strategy. If on the other hand, you've found yourself unable to complete your list on any given day, only to have to re-write parts of the list (or even the whole thing) the next day, then you may realize that the traditional to-do list can be somewhat difficult to stick with. The problem is that days are often unpredictable. Life is a constant balance between competing external inputs such as friends asking you for coffee, your favourite television show coming on, social media distractions, phone calls, or getting sick, and tasks you have for yourself such as getting your assignment done or improving your public speaking skills. In addition, many people's to-do lists don't actually contain action items but are rather listed as projects. This is a classic shortcoming of many to-do lists. You might write "work on sociology paper" or even just "sociology paper" as an item and schedule it in for 11:00 a.m.

on Tuesday. However, written this way, there is no information about what you actually have to do at 11:00 a.m.! It's a flawed approach. You need to invest too much effort figuring out what the task requires during the time you're supposed to be executing the task! Avoiding this effort is a key factor in procrastination.

Project/Task Lists and Specific Action Lists

Instead of falling into the trap of the same to-do list being erased from Monday and being re-written for Tuesday (sound familiar?), consider trying an alternative approach. In this approach, you create a master list of all the projects/tasks you have on. I mean all the projects/tasks—it is extremely liberating when you literally empty your head of all the things you have pending and get them down on a master list. You can offload everything from all aspects of your life onto this list—don't think it's just for school work.

Once you have this master list, you need to think very carefully about what you need to do *next* for each project or task, and then create a sub-list (or even an entirely separate list) which has the *specific pending action* indicated on it. Microsoft Excel or Google spreadsheets, or a table in Microsoft Word or in Pages can help with this list making, as can many other really cool newer apps that are mostly free or inexpensive. I provide details of my favourite apps and packages for making and maintaining lists later on in the chapter. First, let's think about the nature of lists a little more. In his classic time management book David Allen calls projects "open loops"—a term I really like as it conveys the notion that things are incomplete and that *action* is required to close the loop (Allen, 2002). It is useful to set aside a reasonably large chunk of time each week or even twice a week to go through your project list, make sure it is fully up to date, and more importantly, make sure you have identified and written down the specific next actions you need to take to move the project closer to completion.

Scheduling: Deciding How to Use Your Time

How do you currently allocate your time? Let's say it's Monday, the only day this week you don't have classes and you have an anthropology mid-term coming up in two weeks, a psychology research proposal due in three weeks, an aboriginal history seminar the day after tomorrow, a scholarship application due at the end of the week, and some data analysis that you need to present at a lab meeting in one week. You also have been meaning to call your best friend to arrange a time to meet in the break, update your Facebook photos, read up on statistics to improve your understanding, and organize your desk which has been becoming messier and messier lately. Do you do something like what's indicated in Table 6.1 below?

While this list could work, there are other approaches to consider which take into account some of the things we've been talking about but also include an additional step that can help you be a bit more systematic with scheduling. Once you have a list of projects/tasks and a list of pending specific actions for each project, go through your list and write the date by which the project needs to be finished and the approximate time you think it will take to finish. You should then think hard about the next action required for each project and, based on an honest assessment of past experience, you can estimate the time each next action will take. Bear in mind that we usually tend to think things will take less time than they will (this is called the "planning fallacy" in the

Table 6.1 A Typical To-Do List Organized by Time

Monday	Activity
9:00 a.m.	Study for anthropology mid-term
10:00	Check out scholarship form
11:00	Read chapter for aboriginal history class
12:30 p.m.	Call best friend
1:00	Lunch
2:00	Data analysis for lab meeting
3:00	Work on psychology research proposal
4:30	Tidy desk
6:00	Dinner
7:00	Relax/Facebook photos
9:00	Read up on stats

Table 6.2 Master Project List

Project/Task and Total Time Needed	Due Date	Specific Next Action	Time Needed for Next Action	Importance (higher, lower)	Urgency (higher, lower)
Study for anthropology mid-term (10 hours)	2 weeks from now	Read through notes for lectures 2–4, highlight important concepts, and read more on these concepts from the textbook	3 hours	higher	lower
Complete and submit scholarship form (1 hour)	4 days from now	Download form and make a list of supporting documentation needed	30 minutes	higher	higher
Read chapter for aboriginal history seminar (2 hours)	2 days from now	Make notes on chapter and think three questions for discussion in the seminar	2 hours	lower	higher
Data analysis for lab meeting (2 hours)	1 week from now	Make a flow diagram of how to get from the raw data to a summary graph	1 hour	higher	lower
Psychology paper (21 hours)	3 weeks from now	Brainstorming session on the topic	2 hours	higher	lower
Read up on statistics (3 hours)	Whenever, this term	Go through chapter on ANOVA	3 hours	higher	lower
Call best friend about break (30 minutes)	1 month from now	Call Jon	30 minutes	higher	lower
Update Facebook photos	Whenever, this term	Pick photos and upload to FB	1 hour	lower	lower
Tidy desk	As soon as possible	File papers, throw away junk	30 minutes	lower	higher

psychological literature), so a good idea is to add at least 10 per cent more time onto your best guess for each next action.

One useful approach is to enter all this information into a master table as illustrated in Figure 6.2. Once you have the information entered into a table, you can create a priority matrix and assign a priority zone for each task within that matrix (see below).

First, here's a table with all the relevant information shown.

From the table above, you can use the importance and urgency ratings to construct a priority matrix:

Table 6.3 Priority Matrix

		Urgency	
		High	Low
Importance	High	Scholarship form *Priority zone 1*	Anthropology revision Psychology paper Data analysis Call Jon Read stats *Priority zone 2*
	Low	Aboriginal history Tidy desk *Priority zone 3*	Facebook photos *Priority zone 4*

You do not necessarily have to construct a table for this exercise. You could also use any one of apps and programs available on Macs and PCs that create to-do lists. In the next section I outline some useful tools to help with this process.

The importance and urgency levels you assign should be based on your overall goals, and it is easy to see how such a scoring system could differ between individuals with different goals. For example, if you are the kind of person that cannot work on a cluttered desk, you may have designated the "tidy desk" task a high importance and high urgency job, in which case it would be slotted into the priority zone 1. Note also that, with this general approach, theoretically you could be as fine grained as you want to be, by having three or more levels of importance and three or more levels of urgency. Conversely, if you feel that using this quadrant-based approach to visualize priorities is too much hassle, you can always come up with an intuitive priority and include it in the table. In this case, you wouldn't even need the columns depicting importance and urgency in your table. You would replace them with a single column labelled "priority" and you can assign a number to that column (perhaps a scale of one to three, or one to five). This way, you can group projects into clusters by priority level. I don't believe in *one* right way to organize the priorities of your different projects, as the best way really depends on your individual circumstances. What is important in this approach, though, is to have a list of projects, a list of corresponding next actions for each one, and some idea of priority.

Some time management experts highlight the priority zone 2 tasks as the really high impact ones because these are the things that are important but not urgent, and therefore you can really put the time into doing these things very well. These are often long-term planning and thinking tasks, and you should ensure that you set aside ample time for them.

Putting Things into the Calendar

When you've made your table or lists in a software package of your choice (see below for details of my favourite apps and programs for organizing lists), you are ready to start scheduling using your calendar. This is an individual process, and personal work style and preferences must guide how you schedule your time. Let's consider a few ways you could go about scheduling the work described in the table in the preceding section. One approach is to allocate time on your calendar as a function of priority zone. Taking into account your own personal style and your natural daily rhythm (whether you're a morning person or an evening person, for example) is key when deciding how to allocate time. In general, it is a good idea to allocate the most important tasks to times of the day when you are freshest and have the most energy. For most of us, this means not scheduling the most important work for just after lunch! Using the priority zone approach, you might set aside blocks of time for tasks

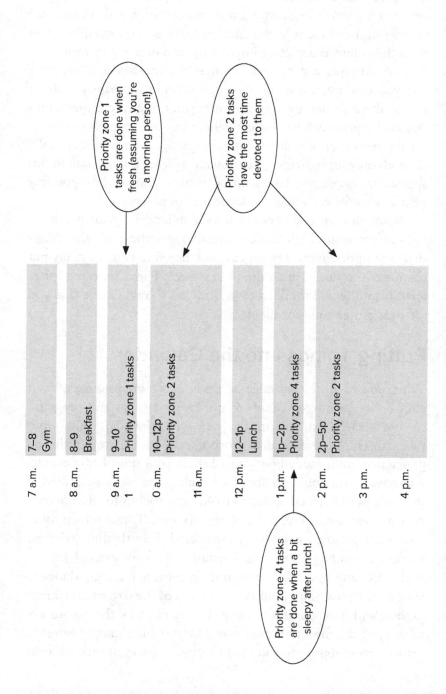

Priority zone 1 tasks are done when fresh (assuming you're a morning person!)

Priority zone 2 tasks have the most time devoted to them

Priority zone 4 tasks are done when a bit sleepy after lunch!

7 a.m.
7–8 Gym

8 a.m.
8–9 Breakfast

9 a.m.
9–10 Priority zone 1 tasks

10 a.m.
10–12p Priority zone 2 tasks

11 a.m.

12 p.m.
12–1p Lunch

1 p.m.
1p–2p Priority zone 4 tasks

2 p.m.
2p–5p Priority zone 2 tasks

3 p.m.

4 p.m.

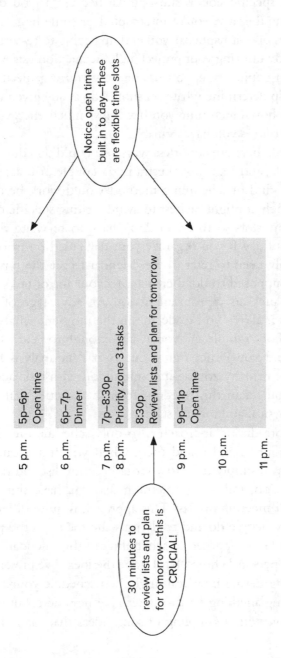

Figure 6.2 Priority Zone Scheduling

Note: You can also include open time slots that are flexible and allow for spontaneous activities like grabbing a coffee or chatting with friends.

within each zone. Note that it is not necessary to enter specific tasks into specific slots unless a particular task absolutely must get done at a particular time (for example, if the task involves someone else and they are only available at a certain time). Otherwise, assigning specific tasks to specific slots is sub-optimal because, if you don't get the task done (because you're interrupted or something more important comes up—it happens), you end up having to re-write it in another slot. By utilizing your project/task/next action lists AND your calendar in conjunction, you have a powerful organizational tool that can help determine what you should do at any given time of day, based on how much time you have, how much energy you have, and the resources you have available.

Bear in mind, there are countless ways you could schedule the work in the table, and I am just illustrating a couple. You are free to decide what kind of scheduling method would work best for you. Again, though, it might be best to avoid writing specific tasks into specific time slots so that you don't have to re-write them for other times of day. If you organize your day based on priority zones, you simply need to refer to the calendar to see the type of activity you're supposed to do, then refer to your list of tasks and next actions to pick an appropriate action. An advantage of this approach is that it allows you to decide in the moment what you feel like doing. For example, are you awake enough to read a long chapter, or would you rather figure out your data analysis flow chart? Using the priority zoning in conjunction with task/action list approach, you retain this freedom to pick activities that suit your current physical and mental state.

Another more drastic approach is to only schedule meetings and classes in your calendar, and then, when you finish one of these activities, you simply refer to your task/action list and time-needed information, and pick something that you have time for before your next meeting or class. This approach is quite different from what many people do and really puts the focus on the project/next action list as opposed to scheduling in the calendar.

Again, it is a personal choice, but I hope the ideas I've presented are useful for considering how you might best schedule your time. I'm not presenting anything Earth-shatteringly new here, but simply providing you with a sampling of some ideas that many have found useful and that have been recommended in time management books on the market. Whatever method you choose, though, be sure to check off completed next actions as you complete them (there are few more satisfying things than crossing off list items!), and review regularly enough to determine the next action for any existing projects or any new projects that have been assigned.

There are ways you can organize your day other than the way illustrated in Figure 6.2. You might be the kind of person who likes to spend extended periods of time on specific projects and focus on only one or two types of task per day, as opposed to mixing task types up. In this case, you might divide your day into two main parts: morning for priority zone 1 tasks and afternoon for priority zone 2 tasks, for example. It really is up to you, and the key is that once you've drawn up your master list you will know what needs to be done by when. There is no single right way to schedule, and different approaches work best for different people. In fact, you may decide that constructing a priority matrix from a table is too much hassle and that it is easier and more effective for you to simply assign priorities intuitively to tasks on your master list. Once you have an idea of what tasks and next steps are priorities, you'll be able to select what to do quite effectively at any given time. Thus, the ideas I am presenting are flexible and can be implemented in multiple ways. So, feel free to experiment with different scheduling approaches until you find one that works best for your own unique style.

Something You Cannot Do Without: Daily and Weekly Reviews

The approach to time management I've described, consisting of project lists and next action lists, only works if the lists you are working with are constantly updated. This means, you need to cross things off as you finish them and add next actions and new projects as they come in. Thus, the main project list with next actions indicated must be an evolving list. I cannot stress enough how your success using this approach depends on the list being up to date and on you reviewing the list so you can anticipate what needs to be done in the coming hours/day. For this reason, I strongly advise putting aside at least 15 minutes daily (either at the end of the day or at the beginning of the day) to review your lists. As in any habit-forming process, you may find it tricky to overhaul your existing planning strategies in favour of a new approach at first, but persistence and patience will help you in effecting change for the better!

Aside from a quick daily review, you should set aside a good amount of time, at least an hour or two on a weekly basis, to review your lists and make sure they are up to date. Lists basically become useless and fade into insignificance if you don't keep them up to date. They also become useless if you just don't do the work and they grow longer and longer day by day. Any system is only useful if it's followed!

The Beauty of Extended Cognition

When human beings first started drawing pictures on cave walls, they suddenly had a way to overcome the limited capacity of their minds. Now, instead of having to remember something, they could draw it on a wall. The wall effectively became an extension of their minds. This notion of representing information externally is referred to as extended cognition. The process of creating a master list of every single thing you need to do is an example of extended cognition. You are taking the load off your memory and thereby freeing yourself up to think more effectively.

If what I've described so far in this chapter seems like work, you're right, it is—especially the construction of project lists and next action lists for each project. This process can take a long time. However, there are important reasons why this up-front work is worth it in the long run. First, don't underestimate the power of writing *every* single outstanding project down and thinking about next actions—this is extended cognition in action and you will feel a weight come off your shoulders when it's done! This process alone liberates you from having to remember things or worse, worry that you've forgotten something vital. I don't know about you, but the feeling that I've forgotten something critical creates mental tension and "brain fog" that I could do without. Second, when you don't have to begin your work session by figuring out what to do, but instead can dive straight into the actual work, your efficiency increases manyfold. Third, when you have a list of actions and estimated time for completion of each action, you can be opportunistic in finishing small tasks in the bits of time you often find here and there. However, as I mentioned, this approach only works if you commit to it and update and review frequently.

Something You Cannot Do Without: Constant Access to Your Organizational Information

Another crucial aspect to implementing the methods I've highlighted is accessibility of your lists and calendar. Thankfully, gone are the days of recommending a paper-based planner: I don't think I've met a single student in the last few years who didn't have a smart phone, tablet, or laptop with them at all times. In a way, this generation of students is blessed with amazing technology that can really help with keeping on top of work and making sure things get done well and on time. Whether you use a Mac or a PC, there are very good apps and software packages that can facilitate your planning and time management. My two favourite general organizational apps are Microsoft OneNote (www.onenote.com) and Evernote (www.evernote.com). These apps both run on Macs and PCs (and Android devices) and allow you to create notebooks in which you can write notes and import web clippings, sound files, photos, videos, PDFs, to-do lists, and other elements. A good approach is to have a dedicated notebook for your master list of projects, tasks, actions, and due dates and then other notebooks for each course you are taking. OneNote and Evernote are basically one-stop shops for all your planning, time management, organizational, note-taking, and work needs. When used in conjunction with your preferred calendar and mind-mapping software, both apps enable immense efficiency and productivity. Another app called DropTask (www.droptask.com) is also excellent. It allows you to create visually appealing task lists and uses icons to indicate the importance and urgency you have assigned for each task. This app also allows for sharing and collaboration. Although it doesn't have the power and flexibility of OneNote or Evernote as a complete one-stop solution, it's definitely worth checking out! One more option that I've come across also deserves mention—it's an app called Todoist (www.todoist.com). I like it because of its simple, clean design and ease of use.

I discussed mind mapping in a previous chapter and am reinforcing how useful mind mapping is for project planning again here. As mentioned in Chapter 2, the best mind mapping software out there (in my opinion) is iMindMap by ThinkBuzan (www.thinkbuzan.com). This software costs approximately $100 for the student edition. If you don't want to fork out that much money, though, there are many free alternatives. One good one that I've seen and that I use is called Coggle (www.coggle.it). However, your options these days are almost endless—there are new apps coming out all the time and I urge you to browse around and experiment with different tools until you find the one that works best for you. If you prefer to consolidate within one environment as opposed to using multiple apps, this is perfectly possible too. If you use Gmail and Google calendar, you can use the task list function to make both your master project/task list and your list of next actions. You can also use the very cool Google Keep app which is perfect for creating project lists with next actions indicated.

Figure 6.3. shows short lists in OneNote, Gmail task list, and Google Keep.

OneNote Project/Next Action List: there are many formats available including a prioritized to-do list. The one shown here is the Project To Do List (there are other available templates). OneNote is the perfect app for busy students. I highly recommend this as the one-stop shop for organizing your life, taking class notes, revising, and basically doing everything you need to do as a student!

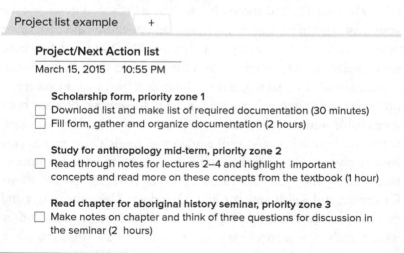

Project list example   +

Project/Next Action list
March 15, 2015   10:55 PM

   Scholarship form, priority zone 1
   ☐ Download list and make list of required documentation (30 minutes)
   ☐ Fill form, gather and organize documentation (2 hours)

   Study for anthropology mid-term, priority zone 2
   ☐ Read through notes for lectures 2–4 and highlight important concepts and read more on these concepts from the textbook (1 hour)

   Read chapter for aboriginal history seminar, priority zone 3
   ☐ Make notes on chapter and think of three questions for discussion in the seminar (2 hours)

Figure 6.3a OneNote Project/Next Action List

Gmail tasks list enables indented lists, perfect for nesting projects with next actions. It is a very simple option if you want to work from within your Gmail environment.

Tasks: Example list for students

☐ **Scholarship form, priority zone 1**   ⟩
    ☐ Download form and make a list of supporting documentation needed—time 30 minutes
    ☐ Fill form, gather and organize documentation—time 2 hours

☐ **Study for anthropology mid-term, priority zone 2**   ⟩
    ☐ Read through notes for lectures 2–4 and highlight important concepts, and read more on these from text—time 1 hour

☐ **Read chapter for aboriginal history seminar, priority zone 3**
    ☐ Make notes on chapter and think of three questions for discussion—time 2 hours

Actions ▶   Pop-in ↙ + 🗑 ☰ ▶

Figure 6.3b Gmail Tasks List

Google Keep: An excellent note and to-do-list app that interfaces with Gmail and Google Calendar. You can set reminders so that you always know what needs doing when.

Add note   ☰

Scholarship form, priority zone 1
☐ Download list and make list of required documentation (30 minutes)
☐ Fill form, gather and organize documentation (2 hours)

Study for anthropology mid-term, priority zone 2
☐ Read through notes for lectures 2–4 and highlight important concepts and read more on these concepts from the textbook (1 hour)

Read chapter for aboriginal history seminar, priority zone 3
☐ Make notes on chapter and think of three questions for discussion in the seminar (2 hours)

Figure 6.3c Google Keep

Of course, there are no "rules" as to how you organize your lists. For example, although in Figure 6.3 next actions are shown under their respective projects, you don't have to take this approach. It is perfectly sensible to have separate lists of projects and next actions. In fact, some people recommend keeping next action lists separate from project lists because not all next actions are part of a larger project (i.e., a next action might be a complete task in itself, whereas a project usually consists of more than one next action). Again, the choice is yours!

Whatever app you pick after testing alternatives, be sure to commit to it. Like anything, all of the ideas presented here and all the tools in the world will be of absolutely no use unless you stick with them. When attempting to use any new organizational system, it is tempting to go back to old habits at first. Take it from me, though, if you persevere through the initial stages, your life will be calmer, more efficient, and *extremely* well organized before you know it! One quick word of caution, though; using technology to help achieve your goals and manage your time effectively is invaluable, but you should be careful not to become so fixated on the technology that you lose sight of the very things that the technology was supposed to help you with!

The Importance of Brainstorming for Project Planning

We've spent considerable time thinking about how you organize your projects and create time slots to do the next actions for each one. However, within a particular project, there may be many next actions necessary to advance you toward your goal. How do you determine what actions are necessary and more importantly, how long the entire project is likely to take? One approach is to brainstorm and mind map all the thoughts that come to mind when you think about your project. When you brainstorm, you should be as open and unedited as possible. Any thought that arises should be aired and written down. Once you've exhausted your thoughts on the topic, go away, take a break, and then come back to the brainstorming session and see if you've missed anything or if anything else springs to mind. You can brainstorm using any

Part of a mindmap brainstorming for a project about obesity in America. Notice that estimated times are indicated for each part. So far, without factoring in integration of the material, preparation of Powerpoint slides, practice, etc., you can see that there are already 9 hours of work involved. Add 10% to the time estimates, just in case, and you have basically 10 hours of work required just to gather information for your project.

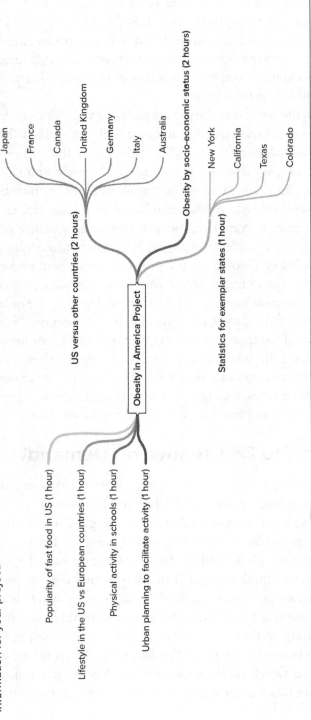

Figure 6.4 Part of a Mind Map for Brainstorming a Project on Obesity in America

approach you like but mind mapping is particularly helpful as it enables you to organize your thoughts hierarchically. During the initial brainstorming phase do not try to organize, though. There may be a natural structure that emerges and that is fine, but don't try to explicitly organize your thoughts, as the sole purpose of the second step is to organize.

In the context of the project planning we've discussed, you could have had a first action for any given project entitled "brainstorming," for which you set aside two hours. At the end of this initial brainstorming session, you can cross off "brainstorming" from your list and list the next action as "organization of brainstorming mind map" and set aside another two hours for this activity. Usually, after this activity is complete, you will be able to visualize all the steps required to complete the project. You may not have specific actions for each step involved in the project, but you will know what the steps are. For example, part of your mind map for a project on obesity in America might be as depicted in Figure 6.4. For each component of the project, you've indicated an estimate for the time needed. This approach can help with figuring out approximately how long the whole project might take. Again, these estimates are just that, and you may find it beneficial to add 10 per cent extra to your time estimates. Figure 6.4 only depicts part of a mind map just to give you an idea of how you might estimate time.

Can You Be Creative on Demand?

Most of this chapter has been concerned with organizing and planning your work, but I'd like to stress something important. Although planning is vital, don't be misguided into the idea that you can always "plan" when you're going to think! Going back to the example I used at the beginning of this chapter, I often find myself thinking while I'm doing something completely unrelated (like golf chipping in the back garden when I was a kid). Nowadays, as a professor who is passionate about the work I do, I am guilty of thinking too much and at very weird times outside of my normal work time! The fact is that humans find it very difficult to switch off their thoughts on demand (try not to think of a white bear). So, if you're working on a project in the afternoon, and have a dinner date in the evening, don't be too hard on yourself if you find yourself distracted by thoughts related to your project. This characteristic of the human mind is a reality that has to be acknowledged: you simply can't plan to be creative or to have that breakthrough idea at a certain time or between 2:00 p.m. and 5:00 p.m. on Wednesday! In view of this, it's important to realize that although it is useful to schedule thinking and planning time (perhaps designated as a priority zone 2 task), you have to organize your life so that you will be able to record great ideas when they arise. Some of my best ideas have come to me in the middle of the night and I've had to get up and write them down. In today's world you are lucky to have technology to help you out when thoughts arise unexpectedly. For example, if you have thoughts or inspiration as you're walking home from university, you can easily use iPhone's Siri (or the Android equivalent) to make voice notes, or simply stop and send yourself a quick email. You can use apps like Onenote and Evernote as "capturing tools" where you store anything that might need your attention at some point. In this way, if you carry a smartphone, you will always have access to a quick and easy way of storing anything that arises (thoughts, requests, emails, or other incoming tasks). Once you have things captured, you can allocate as projects and next actions at a later time, perhaps during a daily or weekly review session. To round out this section, I want to stress that, despite the importance of planning and scheduling (and it really is important), many of the most interesting and useful thoughts you'll have simply cannot be scheduled. So, don't let the idea of planning and scheduling turn you into a robot in search of optimal efficiency. Let yourself be the natural person that you are, but just impose some structure to help make sure the things that need to get done have the best chance at getting done on time.

Planning and List Making Are Half the Equation; The Other Half Is Doing!

The fanciest and most well-organized plans in the world will be completely ineffectual in helping you reach your goals unless you actually *execute* all the necessary steps. You could plan the most optimal day possible but if you decide to go shopping all day instead, it won't work out. Procrastination is something we all suffer from and it can be extremely difficult to overcome. If you find yourself sitting at your desk only to quickly get up to make a coffee, or just focusing on easy priority zone 4 jobs instead of your priority zone 1 and 2 jobs, or looking for other things to do when you're supposed to be focusing on important next actions, you are procrastinating. Don't fret, we all do it—as esteemed psychologist Roy Baumeister highlights in his book *Willpower*, authored with John Tierney, modern surveys show that 95 per cent of people say they procrastinate (and that's just those who admit it!).

Some of the techniques we've talked about in this chapter will themselves reduce your tendency to procrastinate. For example, a common reason for procrastinating is that people feel overwhelmed by the magnitude of the project ahead of them. However, once they've broken down the project into manageable specific actions, that feeling of being overwhelmed quickly dissipates, making it more likely you'll approach the task at hand rather than avoid it. So, the "next specific action" approach is a huge tool in your arsenal against procrastination. A large body of research by Roy Baumeister and his colleagues suggests that the willpower to stick to a task depends on a limited supply of energy and that, when that energy is low, or *depleted* to use Baumeister's term, willpower suffers. In a nutshell, you're less likely to be able to stay on task when you're depleted. Based on this, you should try to get to critical tasks at times when you are not in this sub-optimal state. Another piece of good advice when it comes to avoiding procrastination is not to wait for the perfect amount of time to get something done—you can make a start on something even when you don't have enough time to finish it. For example, when I first started teaching in university, after class, I found myself with a 30-minute time slot before my next appointment. For a full year, I avoided doing anything useful in that 30-minute slot because I used to tell myself that 30 minutes wasn't enough time to get any "real" work done. I soon realized, though, that using that 30 minutes was the difference between making *some progress* toward a goal, and making *no progress* toward a goal. Waiting for the perfect time slot can leave you waiting a long time and is one of the professional procrastinator's most effective strategies for *not* getting work done!

Other useful techniques to avoid procrastination include imagining the negative consequences of not doing a particular action/task. Research shows that anticipating negative consequences can be a strong motivator for helping you act appropriately. For example, anticipated emotions like regret can be helpful in promoting action to avoid the negative experience. In addition, thinking about how working on a project now will help move you toward your longer-term goals is a great way to motivate yourself to seize the moment. Rewards are also a helpful way of motivating yourself to tackle a task—allow yourself a delicious treat or chill-out time with friends after a particularly daunting task. In fact, don't wait until the end of a project to reward yourself, but give yourself smaller rewards as you complete each specific action (or even part action) along the way. Re-evaluate how boring or uninteresting the task at hand actually is. Often, tasks you think are particularly unpleasant are actually not that bad. Create a neat, clean, and uncluttered work environment. Research shows that self-discipline is better maintained in a calm, neat environment rather than a messy, disorganized one. In today's world, it is especially important to give yourself completely uninterrupted time slots to focus on specific tasks. When I say completely uninterrupted, I mean it. You may think you can focus on a task while simultaneously keeping an eye on your email, Facebook, Twitter, and other websites you use, but this is an illusion. Sometimes, you need to fully shield yourself from those distractions to get quality work done. As recommended by renowned dissertation coach Alison Miller, try committing to small chunks of distraction-free (including cellphone free) time—even 25-minute slots can help. Tasks that you avoid become more approachable if they are broken into small chunks of time. If you have trouble refraining from online distractions, consider using software programs such as Freedom (www.freedom.to), that can block access to the most distracting sites for specified time windows. Keep track of your progress on projects, preferably in a way you can depict visually. This simple tip can help motivation. Just as tracking (or charting) weight loss every day can motivate you to stick to your workout and diet goals, so can tracking your progress on work projects. Ultimately though, it is my strong personal experience that the worst procrastination that

I've indulged in has been due to insufficient planning and having an incomplete idea of what I need to do next. To get around this, you should revamp your planning activities so that large overwhelming tasks are always represented in terms of the next specific action required. You can go a long way to beating procrastination by providing yourself with an environment that encourages rather than discourages focused work. Good luck!

Other Things You May Find Helpful

Of course, it would be possible to write a whole book about how to increase your productivity, time management, and efficiency, but in this single chapter I've attempted to provide just some of the most popular and celebrated techniques, with my own insights and modifications added. The basics really are very easy, and by far the hardest part is the breaking of old habits and keeping up with your lists. Take it from me, watching items get crossed off your master list can become quite addictive! Another interesting idea that I've found useful over the years but that I didn't cover in detail in the preceding sections is the 80/20 rule. I am going to mention it here, just as food for thought, and if it sounds intriguing, I recommend you read Richard Koch's book entitled *The 80/20 principle*. Roughly stated, this principle states that 80 per cent of your achievements, happiness, and positive outcomes come from 20 per cent of your activities. Flipped the other way, this means that 80 per cent of your activities are only contributing to 20 per cent of your positive outcomes. Sometimes, it is helpful to analyze your life on the basis of this 80/20 principle and identify the 20 per cent of activities that give you the best outcomes. The implications for time management involve doing more of the 20 per cent activities and less of the 80 per cent of activities that produce less positive outcomes. This sometimes means getting rid of low-value activities altogether, which can be transformational. Remember, the 80/20 principle is not a fact and doesn't always apply. It is, however, a useful idea to consider when organizing your life and deciding how you should set goals, prioritize projects, and allocate time.

The tips and suggestions in this chapter are meant to help you become more productive and increase your efficiency by making the best use of available time. These methods are useful not just for planning and achieving your goals in university; they can equally well be applied to your goals in other areas of your life as well.

Recommended Further Reading

Allen, D. (2001). *Getting things done: The art of stress-free productivity.* New York, NY: Penguin.

Baumeister, R.F., and Tierney, J. (2011). *Willpower: Rediscovering the greatest human strength.* New York, NY: Penguin.

Berk, R. (2009). *The five-minute time manager for college students.* USA: Coventry Press.

Carson, T. (2015). *Work simply: Embracing the power of your personal productivity style.* New York, NY: Penguin.

Koch, R. (2008). *The 80/20 principle: The secret to achieving more with less.* New York, NY: Doubleday.

Appendix 1

Sample Presentation

Slide 1

> ## Effect of tattoos on perceptions of credibility & attractiveness
>
> Seiter, J. & Hatch, S. (2005)
> *Psychological Reports*, 96, 1113–1120
>
> Presented by A.V.G. Student

I'll be talking about this study that looked at how tattoos affect perceptions of credibility and attractiveness.

Slide 2

First Impressions

Quick (< 1 sec) can be based on many things including:

Clothes   Cosmetics   Piercings

  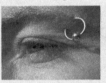

Appearance & dress more important than
interview skills training! (Riggio & Throck-Morten, 1988)

- *First impressions are important:*
- *competence judgments made from a 1 sec exposure predict election outcomes better than chance*
- *Based on things, for example:*
  - *Clothes: Seiter & Dunn (2000)—judgments of how likely person is to be harassed based on looks*
  - *Cosmetics*
  - *Body piercing: Seiter & Sandry (2002)—judgments of hireability (for a male) decreased when he wore a nose ring*
- *Riggio & Throck-Morten study:*
  - *students received one lecture of skills training (interview) and then took part in a videotaped interview*
  - *Raters judging interview performance rated students more on appearance than their skills training status*

Slide 3

Rising Popularity of Tattoos

Tattoo business — 6th-fastest-growing in the US (Lord, 1997)

10% have a tattoo—US (Gardyn, 2001)

LA Ink on TV (Millions of viewers)

- *Tattoo parlours in every town, multiple locations*
- *1997 – tattooing 6th-fastest-growing retail business in the US (interestingly, in a 2011 piece in* Money magazine, *Hyatt noted that up to 20% of tattoo wearers feel regret—nowadays there's a growing demand for tattoo removal too!)*
- *2001, Gardyn reported 10% of people in the US have a tattoo—more by now*
- *2010 study by Koch et al found 14% of US college students had tattoos (>1700 data points)*
- *Newer data (Dickson et al, 2014 puts that number at about 20%)*
- *Interest in tattoos exemplified by TV shows – e.g., LA Ink, Inked*

Slide 4

Historical Negative Associations

West: Perverts, psychopaths, prostitutes and psychotics (Forbes, 2001)

Women with tattoos rated: less attractive, more promiscuous, and heavier drinkers than non-tattooed (Swami & Furnham, 2007)

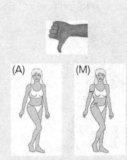

- *Historically, tattoos were signs that a person wanted to be "out of the mainstream"*
- *Example, prisoners got tattooed in jail*
- *Forbes (2001) notes that tattoos have been associated with antisocial groups for most of the last century*
- *2007 study Swami & Furnham found that line drawings of women with and without tattoos were rated differently with tattooed women rated as:*
  - *Less attractive*
  - *More promiscuous*
  - *Heavier drinkers than non-tattooed women*
- *Koch et al. (2010)—college sample individuals with tattoos had increasing tendency to cheat on college work, binge drink, and be more promiscuous*
- *People with 4+tattoos found to have increased drug usage and greater history of being arrested for a crime*

Slide 5

Tattoos and Person Perception

Woman with tattoo rated LESS: Attractive

Intelligent

Artistic

Athletic

Motivated

Generous

Mysterious

Religious

Honest

(Degelman & Price, 2002)

- *Degelman and Price asked college and high school students to rate a photo of a woman with or without a tattoo*
- *They rated them on 13 characteristics:*
  - *Fashionable, athletic, attractive, caring, creative, determined, motivated, honest, generous, mysterious, religious, intelligent, artistic*
- *Women with the tattoo were rated lower on 9 of these characteristics*
- *Not related to whether rater had or did not have a tattoo*
- *Black and white photo is the ACTUAL stimulus used by these authors*
- *Students were from schools in California*

Slide 6

Reduces Employability

Employers less likely
to hire person with tattoo
(Bekhor et al., 1995)

- *Several previous studies examined perception with respect to tattoos*

Slide 7

> # Questions and Hypothesis
>
> **Question:**
> What are the effects of tattoos on peceptions
> of attractiveness and competence?
>
> **Hypothesis:**
> *People will perceive males and females*
> *with tattoos as significantly less credible*
> *and attrctive than people without tattoos*

- *So, to transition to the actual research question and hypothesis:*
  - *Researchers were generally interested in the effects of tattoos on perceptions of attractiveness and competence*
  - ***Specific hypothesis*** *was that people will perceive others with tattoos as less credible and less attractive than people without tattoos.*

Slide 8

Method

Participants shown one of four different photos:

	Male Model	Female Model
With tattoo	1	2
Without tattoo	3	4

Participants were undergrads in an Intro Communications course, who filled out questionnaire relating to a photograph of a model given to them

Volunteer models were a 22-year-old male student and a 22-year-old female student

They were photographed with or without a:
- Black decorative tattoo band

Location of tattoo was on:
- Tattoo location left upper arm (used photo editing software to add tattoo)

They wore:
- Jeans, black t-shirt, neutral facial expression

For photo they:
- Faced camera and turned body 45 degrees

Slide 9

Measures

7-point Likert scales to rate:

Competence Attractiveness

- *Total participants:*
- *148*
- *Four groups*
- *Each participant rated the model's perceived competence and attractiveness using two established scales*
- *They used a Likert scale for rating—this is just a numerical scale with numbers from 1 to 7, where 1 is very low and 7 is very high*

Slide 10

Competence

Source Credibility scale, 15 items, 5 dimensions:

- Competence
- Character
- Sociability
- Extroversion
- Composure

(McCroskey, Hamilton, & Weiner, 1974)

- *Competence was assessed by the Source Credibility scale which consists of 15 items and 5 dimensions:*
- *The individual dimensions were:*
  - *Competence*
  - *Character*
  - *Sociability*
  - *Extroversion*
  - *Composure*

Slide 11

Attractiveness

Interpersonal Attraction Scale, 3 dimensions:

- Physical attraction
- Social attraction
- Task attraction

- *The attractiveness scale is previously validated and has three dimensions*
- *Physical attraction*
- *Social attraction measures how easy someone is to get on with*
- *Task attraction measures how well someone can get the job done*

Slide 12

Results

Table 1 Means and Standard Deviations for Credibility and Atraction by Presence of Tattoo and Sex (*N* = 74)

Measure	No Tattoo				Tattoo			
	Men		Women		Men		Women	
	M	*SD*	*M*	*SD*	*M*	*SD*	*M*	*SD*
Credibility								
Competence	4.4	1.2	4.7	1.0	4.2	1.0	4.1	1.0
Character	4.9	1.1	5.2	1.0	4.6	0.8	4.4	1.2
Sociability	5.0	1.1	4.5	0.9	4.8	1.0	4.1	1.1
Extroversion	3.9	1.3	3.2	1.1	4.5	1.3	3.9	1.3
Composure	4.5	1.3	3.9	1.1	4.7	1.4	3.9	1.2
Attraction								
Social	4.9	1.2	4.7	1.0	4.7	1.3	4.9	1.1
Physical	5.1	1.7	5.8	1.2	5.1	1.3	5.4	1.3
Task	4.6	1.2	5.2	0.9	4.6	1.1	5.0	1.0

- *Authors conducted a multivariate analysis of variance in a 2 Presence of tattoo: (tattoo, no tattoo) x 2 model gender: (male model, female model)*
- *Found main effects for both factors.*
- *Main analysis was a series of univariate tests (Student-Newman-Keuls post hoc tests)*
- *They presented their results in a table like this, which is a little tricky to decipher.*
- *I TRANSLATED THE MAIN RESULTS INTO GRAPHS TO SHOW YOU WHAT THEY FOUND!*
- *GRAPHS THAT I WILL SHOW YOU ARE BASED ON THE DATA IN THE TABLE AND ARE COLLAPSED ACROSS THE MALE AND FEMALE MODEL CONDITIONS*

Slide 13

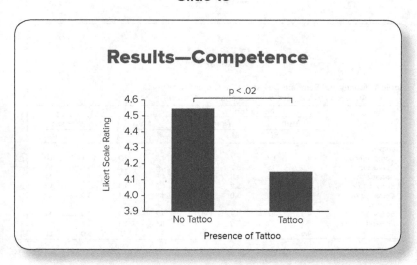

As you can see:

- Models without a tattoo were rated as significantly more competent than those with a tattoo!

Slide 14

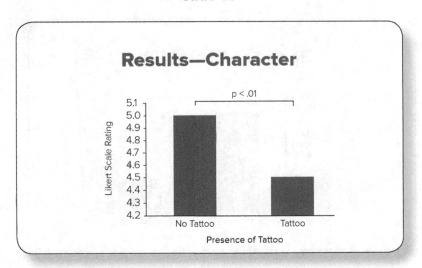

As you can see here,

- *Models with no tattoo rated higher on the character dimension compared to those with a tattoo*

Slide 15

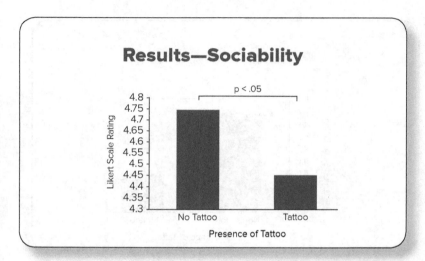

- *Models without a tattoo were also rated higher on sociability compared to those without a tattoo*

Slide 16

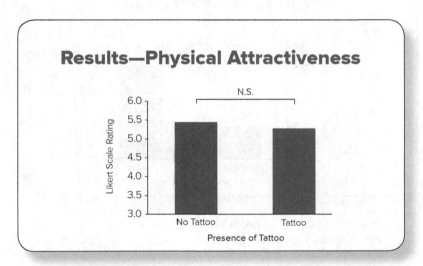

- *VERY INTERESTING*
- *NO differences found in attractiveness—here I show the results for the Physical Attractiveness dimension*
- *BUT*
- *No differences for Social or Task attractiveness either!*
- *So tattoos DO NOT appear to make you more attractive to others*

Slide 17

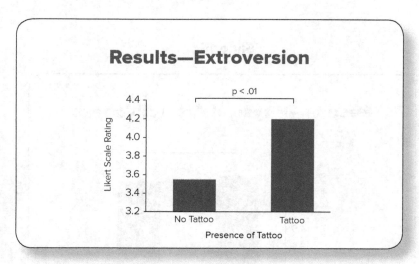

- *The one dimension on which models with a tattoo scored higher than those without was EXTROVERSION*
- *Not really surprising*

Slide 18

Conclusions

- Tattoo harms more than helps perceptions of competence

- Tatoo did not affect attractiveness ratings

Why?
- – Conservative appearance = competence

(Seiter & Sandry, 2003)

- To conclude, this paper showed:
  - Visible tattoos HURT perceptions of competence
  - Tattoos DO NOT make you more attractive either
- SO, in essence, a double disaster for tattoos!
- WHY IS THIS?
- Same author previously showed that:
  - Nose or ear piercings as less hirable and credible than the same model shown without a piercing (NOSE PIERCING = BIGGER EFFECT)
- Therefore:
  - Credibility and competence (important component of hirability) are rated higher when people are more conservatively dressed
  - Role theory—people have normative expectations of what a job candidate looks like; violations are negatively appraised
- Interesting: participants comprised STUDENTS and MANAGERS and results were the same
- Bringing the focus back to this study:
  - Tattoos are not conservative!!

Slide 19

Critique

- **Stimulus**
  - Only used one type of tattoo
- **Measures**
  - Explicit measure only, what about effects on implicit measures?
- **Method**
  - No context for ratings of competence
- **Paper**
  - Paper lacked detail—NOT replicable
  - No graphs in the paper, no exact p-values
  - Limitations not adequately discussed

- *Study very simple and interesting*
- *Popular topic*
- *SEVERAL major criticisms of the research and paper:*
  1. *Stimulus set was VERY LIMITED—ONLY USED ONE TYPE OF TATTOO*
  2. *EXPLICIT SELF-REPORT MEASURES WERE ONLY ONES*
     - *What about implicit measures of stigma or prejudice?*
  3. *DOESN'T TALK ABOUT CONTEXT*
     - *presumably, appraisals are made within some kind of social context*
     - *the authors didn't give a context to participants—so not sure exactly what participants were considering*
  4. *In terms of the paper:*
     - *Lacked detail—should have included the questionnaire as an appendix—method as reported is NOT COMPLETELY REPLICABLE*
     - *Didn't report exact p-values and didn't comment on the main effects from the MANOVA*
     - *Should have used graphs to depict the main results*
  5. *No extensive discussion of limitations*
     - *What do the results mean? Do the effects disappear the moment the person opens their mouth? Are they only first impressions?*
- *Real-world significance?*
  - *If offset the tattoo with other info about COMPETENCE—like for example A RESUME, would effects disappear?*
- *These are all obvious and important questions that could have at lease been discussed in the pape.*
- *Overall, I would give this paper a 7/10 (my own rating scale)*
- *It was interesting, simple and informative, but extremely limited and hard to extend to real life*

Slide 20

Take-home Message

To be seen as:

Competent

Attractive

. . . or at least cover it up!

- *This study is one of a few now that have shown negative effects of tattoos on person perception*
- *So, like most people, if you want to be seen as competent and attractive*
- *Think before you ink*
- *Or just make sure you can cover it up!!!*

Sample Research Paper

Getting Along: Mimicry in Social Interactions
A.V.G. Student
University Name Here [1]

1. Running head is an APA recommendation. This title page conforms to APA style guidelines.

Social Psychology 201
Professor V. Good
March 20th 2015

The old woman unfolds her arms and moments later her husband unfolds his arms. She scratches her chin, he scratches his chin. They look so happy sitting there in the café drinking coffee. She smiles, he smiles. On closer analysis, you see that their faces are actually quite similar; they have the same wrinkle lines. What on earth is going on?[2] Human beings are intensely social and good quality human contact is known to contribute to positive health outcomes. Conversely, bad relationships are associated with negative effects on health and happiness. It is thought that couples that have been happily married for a long time start to look similar due to the formation of similar wrinkle lines, caused by mimicking each other's facial expressions. High-quality social relationships such as those we have with people we like are characterized by feelings of rapport, smoothness, and ease. Why is this? What is it about good social interactions that gives us these warm, fuzzy feelings? As the old happy couple mentioned above illustrate, mimicking each other is a natural tendency associated with good social relationships. Mimicry can involve copying the gestures, facial expressions, speech tones, or other bodily movements of a social interaction partner. Researchers in the domain of social psychology have studied mimicry quite extensively and have identified many factors that increase and decrease it, as well as some of its social consequences. Although social interactions are complex, social mimicry appears to be a key element in why we experience positive feelings when interacting with people we like.[3]

You may have caught yourself scratching your chin in the middle of a conversation with a friend, only to realize that sev-

---

2. Create a hook—who is this old woman? Turn this into a question and a broad consideration of humans as social beings. Then narrow down to mimicry as a tool for building rapport.

3. This is essentially a thesis statement highlighting that you'll be talking about what researchers know about mimicry. Make sure the following paragraphs do this!

eral seconds earlier your friend had scratched their chin. You usually catch yourself mimicking your friend *after* you've performed the action, suggesting that the actual copying is initiated unconsciously.[4] This assertion is supported by evidence showing that experimental participants unintentionally mimic an interaction partner even when that partner is a stranger. In a now classic study, Chartrand & Bargh (1999) found that participants who interacted with a foot-shaking confederate performed more foot shakes than face touches, and participants who interacted with a face-touching confederate performed more face touches than foot shakes. Furthermore, participants who were mimicked by the confederate rated the interaction as going more smoothly than those who were not mimicked, and reported increased liking for the confederate (see Chartrand & Lakin, 2013 for similar results).[5] Thus, mimicry occurs even between strangers and leads to a positive appraisal of the interaction.[6] Taken together, these studies show that mimicry is moderated by a host of factors and is involved in the attainment of social affiliation goals.[7]

4. Nice example to help appreciate the issue at hand.

5. Followed by 1–2 punch approach : single citation and review paper to back it up

6. This paragraph highlights factors that affect mimicry.

7. Summarize the paragraph simply.

Mimicry has also been found to exert effects beyond the dyadic interaction in which it occurs. Research has demonstrated that participants who have been mimicked by a confederate display more prosocial behaviour after the interaction than participants who have not been mimicked. Prosocial behaviour, in contrast to antisocial behaviour, is behaviour that benefits others and that is co-operative. In one study, after a social interaction, the experimenter "accidentally" dropped lots of pens in the vicinity of the participant. Participants who had been recently mimicked picked up more pens than participants who had not been recently mimicked (van Baaren, Holland, Kawakami, & van Knippenberg, 2004). Being mimicked then, apparently leads to greater helping behaviour than not being mimicked. A compelling demonstration of increased prosocial behaviour is the finding that participants who have just been mimicked make more donations to charity than those who have not just been mimicked (Stel, van Baaren, & Vonk, 2008).[8] Hence, across multiple studies, mimicry is associated with prosocial effects that extend beyond the dyad in which the mimicry occurred.[9]

8. This paragraph focuses on the effects of mimicry beyond the social interaction in which it occured.

9. Summarize the paragraph simply.

Social mimicry seems to occur without conscious intent and therefore has a key hallmark of an automatic tendency. But what are the origins of this ubiquitous behavioural tendency? Although the current state of knowledge in this field precludes a full answer to this question, some have speculated that mimicry has endured because of its adaptive value in our evolutionary past. In particular, as early humans began living in ever more complex social groups, the importance of forming and maintaining good social relationships became increasingly important. It is possible that through its positive effects on rapport and liking, mimicry helped address this important need (Lakin, Jefferies, Cheng, & Chartrand, 2003). The suggestion then, is that evolution favoured social mimicry due to its efficacy in forming and maintaining the kinds of good social relationships that were key to co-operative group living.[10]

10. This paragraph focuses on the potential origins of mimicry and at the end, a sentence summarizes the main idea again.

In summary, fulfilling social interactions are linked to health and happiness and one social tendency thought to underlie good social interactions is mimicry. In this paper, just a fraction of the fascinating work on social mimicry has been discussed. This work suggests that mimicry is a powerful unconsciously initiated behaviour that helps create smooth social interactions with others. Mimicry is strategic in the sense that it is triggered unconsciously in response to experiences such as social exclusion. It is also associated with a wide range of prosocial behaviours that extend beyond the social interaction in which it occurred. Finally, mimicry may have endured due to its efficacy in promoting harmonious social relationships in our ancestral past.[11] So, the next time you are in a social interaction that isn't going well, try mimicking the person you're talking with. You never know, you might become best friends.[12]

11. Use "In summary" to underline that this is the last paragraph. Briefly re-state the main focus and then summarize the primary ideas introduced above.

12. Final two sentences are back to an example from everyday life (implications of some of the research discussed above). The very last sentence is short and punchy.

References

Chartrand, T. L., & Bargh, J. A. (1999). The chameleon effect: The perception–behavior link and social interaction. *Journal of Personality and Social Psychology*, 76(6), 893–910. doi: 10.1037/0022-3514.76.6.893

Chartrand, T.L., & Lakin, J.I. (2013). The antecedents and consequences of human behavioral mimicry. *Annual Review of Psychology*, 64, 285–308. doi: 10.1146/annurev-psych-113011-143754

Lakin, J. L., Jefferis, V. E., Cheng, C. M., & Chartrand, T. L. (2003). The chameleon effect as social glue: Evidence for the evolutionary significance of nonconscious mimicry. *Journal of Nonverbal Behavior*, 27(3), 145–162. doi: 10.1023/A:1025389814290

van Baaren, R. B., Holland, R. W., Kawakami, K., & van Knippenberg, A. (2004). Mimicry and prosocial behavior. *Psychological Science*, 15(1), 71–74. doi: 10.1111/j.0963-7214.2004.01501012.x

Stel, M., Van Baaren, R. B., & Vonk, R. (2008). Effects of mimicking: Acting prosocially by being emotionally moved. *European Journal of Social Psychology*, 38(6), 965–976. doi: 10.1002/ejsp.472

References

Allen, D. (2001). *Getting things done: The art of stress-free productivity.* New York, NY: Penguin.

American Psychological Association. (2010). *Publication manual of the American Psychological Association* (6th ed.). Washington, DC: APA.

Andersen, J.F., & Anderson, P.A. (1987). Never smile until Christmas? Casting doubt on an old myth. *Journal of Thought, 22*(4), 57–61.

Arent, S., & Landers, D. (2003). Arousal, anxiety, and performance: A re-examination of the inverted-U hypothesis. *Research Quarterly for Exercise & Sport, 74*(4), 436–444.

Baker, S., & Gamache, L.B. (1998). *The Canadian practical stylist with readings* (4th ed.). Toronto, ON: Pearson Canada.

Baumeister, R.F. and Tierney, J. (2011). *Willpower: Rediscovering the greatest human strength.* New York, NY: Penguin.

Becker, H.S., & Richards, P. (2007). *Writing for social scientists: How to start and finish your thesis, book, or article.* Chicago, IL: University of Chicago Press.

Beebe, S.A. (1974). Eye contact: A nonverbal determinant of speaker credibility. *The Speech Teacher, 23*(1), 21–25.

Berk, R. (2009). *The five-minute time manager for college students.* USA: Coventry Press.

Burgoon, M. (1990). Language and social influence. In H. Giles & P. Robinson (Eds.), *Handbook of language and social psychology* (pp. 51–72). London: John Wiley & Sons.

Burtis, J. & Turman, P. (2006). *Group communication pitfalls.* Thousand Oaks, CA: Sage Publications.

Buss, A.H. (1980). *Self-consciousness and social anxiety.* San Francisco: Freeman

Carducci, B.J., & Zimbardo, P.G. (1995). Are you shy? *Psychology Today, 28,* 34–41.

Carson, T. (2015). *Work simply: Embracing the power of your personal productivity style.* New York, NY: Penguin.

Cook, M. (1977). Gaze and mutual gaze in social encounters. *American Scientist, 65*(3), 328–333.

Cook, M., & Smith, J.M. (1975). The role of gaze in impression formation. *British Journal of Social & Clinical Psychology, 14*(1), 19–25. doi: 10.1111/j.2044-8260.1975.tb00144.x

Cook, S. W., Mitchell, Z., & Goldin-Meadow, S. (2008). Gesturing makes learning last. *Cognition 106*(2), 1047–1058. doi: 10.1016/j.cognition.2007.04.010

Esposito, J.E. (2007). *In the spotlight: Overcoming your fear of public speaking and performing.* Bridgewater, CT: In the Spotlight, LLC.

Esser, J. (1998). Alive and well after 25 years: A review of Groupthink research. *Organizational Behavior and Human Decision Processes, 73,* 116–141.

Evans, G.E. (1988). Metaphors as learning aids in university lectures. *Journal of Experimental Education, 56*(2), 91–99.

Feldman, D.B., & Silvia, P.J. (2010). *Public speaking for psychologists: A lighthearted guide to research presentations, job talks, and other opportunities to embarrass yourself.* Washington, DC: American Psychological Association.

Feldman, K.A. (1989). The association between student ratings of specific instructional dimensions and student achievement: Refining and extending the synthesis of data from multisection validity studies. *Research in Higher Education, 30*(6), 583–645.

Fredrickson, B.L., & Kahneman, D. (1993). Duration neglect in retrospective evalua-tions of affective episodes. *Journal of Personality and Social Psychology, 65*(1), 45–55.

Fremouw, W.J., & Zitter, R.E. (1978). A comparison of skills training and cognitive restructuring–relaxation for the treatment of speech anxiety. *Behavior Therapy, 9*(2), 248–259. doi: 10.1016/S0005-7894(78)80110-5

Garner, R. (2005). Humor, analogy, and metaphor: H.A.M. it up in teaching. *Radical Pedagogy, 6*(2). Retrieved from http://www.radicalpedagogy.org

Goldin-Meadow, S. (1999). The role of gesture in communication and thinking. *Trends in Cognitive Sciences, 3*(11), 419–429.

Goldin-Meadow, S., Nusbaum, H., Kelly, S.D., & Wagner, S. (2001). Explaining math: Gesturing lightens the load. *Psychological Science, 12*(6), 516–522. doi: 10.1111/1467-9280.00395

Johnson, D.W., & Johnson, R.T. (1989). *Cooperation and competition: Theory and research.* Edina, MN: Interaction Book Company.

Johnson, D.W., & Johnson, R.T. (1998). Cooperative learning and social interdepen-dence theory. In R.S.Tindale (Ed.), *Theory and research on small groups* (pp. 9–35). New York, NY: Plenum Press.

Johnson, D. & Johnson, R. (2009). An educational psychology success story: Social interdependence theory and co-operative learning. *Education and Educational Research, 38*, 365–379.

Koch, R. (2008). *The 80/20 principle: The secret to achieving more with less.* New York, NY: Doubleday.

Kosslyn, S.M. (2007). *Clear and to the point: Eight psychological principles for compelling PowerPoint presentations.* New York, NY: Oxford University Press.

Kosslyn, S.M., Kievit, R.A., Russell, A.G., & Shephard, J.M. (2012). PowerPoint pre-sentation flaws and failures: A psychological analysis. *Frontiers in Psychology, 3* doi: 10.3389/fpsyg.2012.00230

Larson, C.E., & LaFasto, F.M.J. (1989). *Team Work: What must go right/what can go wrong.* Thousand Oaks, CA: Sage Publications.

Matsumoto, D., & Sung Hwang, H. (2013). Body and gestures. In D. Matsumoto & H. Sung Hwang (Eds.), *Nonverbal communication: Science and applications* (pp. 75–96). Thousand Oaks, CA: Sage Publications.

Mayer, R. E., Heiser, J., & Lonn, S. (2001). Cognitive constraints on multimedia learning: When presenting more material results in less understanding. *Journal of Educational Psychology, 93*(1), 187–198. doi: 10.1037/0022-0663.93.1.187

McGinley, H., Nicholas, K., & McGinley, P. (1978). Effects of body position and attitude similarity on interpersonal attraction and opinion change. *Psychological Reports, 42*(1), 127–138. doi: 10.2466/pr0.1978.42.1.127

McKay, M., Davis, M. & Fanning, P. (2011). *Thoughts and feelings: Taking control of your moods and your life* (4th ed.). Oakland, CA: New Harbinger Publications.

Mehrabian, A., & Williams, M. (1969). Nonverbal concomitants of perceived and intended persuasiveness. *Journal of Personality and Social Psychology, 13*, 37–58.

Miller, A. (2009). *Finish your dissertation once and for all: How to overcome psycholog-ical barriers, get results, and move on with your life.* Washington, DC: American Psychological Association.

Miller, F. (2011). *No sweat public speaking: How to develop, practice and deliver a knock your socks off presentation with no sweat.* St. Louis, MO: Fred Co.

Norcross, J.C., Mrykalo, M.S., & Blagys, M.D. (2002). Auld lang syne: Success predictors, change processes, and self-reported outcomes of New Year's resolvers and non-resolvers. *Journal of Clinical Psychology, 58*(4), 397–405. doi: 10.1002/jclp.1151

Northey, M., Tepperman, L., & Albanese, P. (2012). *Making sense: A student's guide to research and writing: Social sciences* (5th ed.). New York, NY: Oxford University Press.

Pilkonis, P.A. (1977). The behavioral consequences of shyness. *Journal of Personality, 45*(4), 596–611.

Pinker, S. (2014). *The sense of style: The thinking person's guide to writing in the 21st century.* New York, NY: Viking.

Reisberg, D. (2012). *Cognition: Exploring the science of the mind* (5th ed.). New York, NY: W.W. Norton.

Reynolds. G. (2012). *Presentation Zen: Simple ideas on presentation design and delivery* (2nd ed.). Berkeley, CA: New Riders.

Rothwell, J.D. (2004). *In mixed company: Communicating in small groups and teams.* Boston, MA: Wadsworth.

Schultz, S. (2009). *Eloquent science: A practical guide to becoming a better writer, speaker and atmospheric scientist.* Boston, MA: American Meteorological Society.

Suzuki, H., & Heath, L. (2014). Impacts of humor and relevance on the remembering of lecture details. *Humor: International Journal of Humor Research, 27*(1), 87–101. doi: 10.1515/humor-2013-0051

Wang, Y. (2014). Humor in British academic lectures and Chinese students' perceptions of it. *Journal of Pragmatics, 68*, 80–93. doi: 10.1016/j.pragma.2014.05.003

Weinberg, R. S., & Gould, D. (1995). *Foundations of sport and exercise psychology.* Champaign, IL: Human Kinetics.

Woolfolk, R.L., Parrish, M.W., & Murphy, S.M. (1985). The effects of positive and negative imagery on motor skill performance. *Cognitive Therapy and Research, 9*(3), 335–341. doi: 10.1007/BF01183852

Credits

Index